JOSHUA BRUCE

How to Ace a Job Interview

A Comprehensive Approach to Mastering Job Interviews and Advancing Your Career

Copyright © 2024 by Joshua Bruce

All rights reserved. No part of this publication may be reproduced, stored or transmitted in any form or by any means, electronic, mechanical, photocopying, recording, scanning, or otherwise without written permission from the publisher. It is illegal to copy this book, post it to a website, or distribute it by any other means without permission.

First edition

This book was professionally typeset on Reedsy.
Find out more at reedsy.com

Contents

Introduction: Your Path to Interview Success	1
Chapter 1: The Psychology of Successful Interviews: Mindset...	6
Chapter 2: First Impressions: Dress, Body Language, and...	18
Chapter 3: Researching the Company: Become an Insider Before...	25
Chapter 4: Crafting Your Personal Brand: Aligning Your Story...	31
Chapter 5: Mastering Common Interview Questions (and Dreaded...	37
Chapter 6: The STAR Method: Structuring Compelling Responses	44
Chapter 7: Showcasing Your Achievements: Quantify Your...	50
Chapter 8: Addressing Employment Gaps and Career Transitions	57
Chapter 9: The Art of Asking Questions: Impress with Your...	64
Chapter 10: Navigating Different Interview Formats:...	71
Chapter 11: Virtual Interviews: Excelling in the Digital...	78
Chapter 12: Behavioral Interviews: Proving You're the...	85
Chapter 13: Technical Interviews: Demonstrating Your...	92
Chapter 14: Salary Negotiations: Knowing Your Worth and...	101
Chapter 15: Following Up: The Post-Interview Strategy That...	108
Chapter 16: Handling Rejection: Turning a 'No' into a Future...	116
Chapter 17: Interview Preparation Checklist: Your...	123
Chapter 18: Industry-Specific Interview Tips: Tailoring Your...	129
Chapter 19: The Power of Mock Interviews: Practice Makes...	136
Chapter 20: Beyond the Job Offer: Evaluating Opportunities...	144
Conclusion	152

Introduction: Your Path to Interview Success

In today's competitive job market, landing your dream job isn't just about having the right qualifications—it's about mastering the art of the interview. Whether you're a recent graduate stepping into the professional world for the first time, a seasoned executive looking to climb higher on the corporate ladder, or someone changing careers entirely, the ability to ace a job interview is an invaluable skill that can dramatically alter the trajectory of your professional life.

"How to Ace a Job Interview" is your comprehensive guide to navigating the often daunting world of job interviews with confidence, poise, and strategic finesse. This book is designed to be your trusted companion, offering insider knowledge, proven techniques, and actionable strategies that will set you apart from other candidates and position you as the ideal choice for any role you aspire to.

Why This Book?

In an era where information is abundant and advice is often just a click away, you might wonder why you need this book. The answer is simple: while there's no shortage of interview tips online, what's lacking is a cohesive, structured approach that takes you from preparation to post-interview follow-up, covering every aspect of the interview process in depth.

This book fills that gap. It's not just a collection of random tips; it's a meticulously crafted roadmap that will guide you through each step of the interview process, helping you to:

1. Understand the psychology behind successful interviews
2. Craft compelling responses that showcase your unique value
3. Navigate different interview formats with ease
4. Handle challenging questions and unexpected scenarios
5. Negotiate your worth confidently
6. Turn even rejections into valuable learning experiences and future opportunities

What Sets This Book Apart

Unlike many interview guides that offer a one-size-fits-all approach, "How to Ace a Job Interview" recognizes that every job seeker is unique. Whether you're an introvert who struggles with self-promotion or an extrovert who needs to learn to listen more, this book provides tailored strategies to play to your strengths and mitigate your weaknesses.

Moreover, this book goes beyond surface-level advice. Instead of just telling you to "be confident" or "do your research," we delve into the how and why behind these suggestions. You'll learn not just what to do, but why it works, empowering you to adapt these strategies to any interview situation you might encounter.

The Changing Landscape of Job Interviews

The world of work is evolving rapidly, and with it, so are job interviews. This book takes into account the latest trends and shifts in hiring practices, including:

INTRODUCTION: YOUR PATH TO INTERVIEW SUCCESS

- The rise of virtual interviews and how to excel in them
- The increasing use of AI in the hiring process and how to navigate it
- The growing importance of soft skills and emotional intelligence
- The shift towards behavioral and situational interviewing techniques

By staying ahead of these trends, you'll be prepared not just for the interviews of today, but for those of tomorrow as well.

What You'll Learn

As you journey through this book, you'll gain insights and practical skills that will transform your approach to job interviews. Here's a glimpse of what you'll discover:

- The psychology of first impressions and how to make yours count
- Techniques for researching companies that go beyond their website
- Strategies for crafting your personal brand and aligning it with potential employers
- The STAR method for structuring powerful, memorable responses
- Tactics for turning your weaknesses into strengths
- Negotiation techniques that help you secure the salary you deserve
- Industry-specific tips that give you an edge in your chosen field

But perhaps most importantly, you'll learn how to approach interviews with a mindset of confidence and authenticity. Because at its core, a great interview isn't about pretending to be someone you're not—it's about presenting the best version of yourself and clearly communicating the unique value you bring to the table.

Who This Book Is For

While "How to Ace a Job Interview" is comprehensive enough for job seekers at any stage of their career, it's particularly valuable for:

- Recent graduates entering the job market for the first time
- Mid-career professionals looking to make a significant career move
- Career changers transitioning to a new industry
- Anyone who has struggled with interviews in the past and wants to improve their skills
- Professionals in highly competitive fields where interview performance can make or break job prospects

How to Use This Book

This book is designed to be both a cover-to-cover read and a reference guide. We recommend starting at the beginning to build a solid foundation of interview skills. However, each chapter is also self-contained, allowing you to jump to specific sections as needed when preparing for an upcoming interview.

The chapters are arranged in a logical sequence that mirrors the interview process itself, from preparation and first impressions through to follow-up and decision-making. Throughout the book, you'll find practical exercises, real-world examples, and expert insights that will help you internalize and apply the strategies discussed.

A Promise and an Invitation

By the time you finish this book, you will approach job interviews not with anxiety, but with excitement. You'll see each interview as an opportunity—not just to land a job, but to learn, grow, and move closer to your career goals.

INTRODUCTION: YOUR PATH TO INTERVIEW SUCCESS

But our journey together doesn't end with the last page of this book. The world of work is constantly evolving, and so too must our strategies for navigating it. That's why we invite you to join our online community of fellow job seekers and career enthusiasts. Here, you can share your experiences, ask questions, and stay updated on the latest interview trends and techniques.

So, are you ready to transform your interview skills and open doors to exciting new opportunities? Let's begin this journey together. Turn the page, and take your first step towards acing your next job interview—and every one after that.

Chapter 1: The Psychology of Successful Interviews: Mindset Matters

The moment you step into an interview room, you're not just presenting your skills and experience—you're engaging in a complex psychological dance. Understanding the psychology behind successful interviews is the foundation upon which all other interview skills are built. In this chapter, we'll explore how your mindset can make or break your interview performance and provide you with strategies to cultivate a winning psychological approach.

The Power of Mindset

Carol Dweck, a renowned psychologist, introduced the concept of growth versus fixed mindsets. In the context of job interviews, adopting a growth mindset—the belief that your abilities can be developed through dedication and hard work—is crucial. This mindset allows you to view the interview as an opportunity for learning and growth, rather than a do-or-die test of your worth.

Cultivating a growth mindset for interviews involves:

1. Embracing challenges: See difficult questions as opportunities to showcase your problem-solving skills.

2. Persisting in the face of setbacks: If you stumble on a question, recover gracefully and move forward.
3. Viewing effort as the path to mastery: Recognize that thorough preparation is key to interview success.
4. Learning from criticism: Use feedback from past interviews to improve your performance.
5. Finding lessons and inspiration in others' success: Study successful interview strategies and adapt them to your style.

The Confidence Conundrum

Confidence is a critical factor in interview success, but it's a delicate balance. Too little confidence can make you appear unsure and incompetent, while overconfidence might come across as arrogance. The key is to project authentic confidence—a quiet assurance in your abilities that's grounded in reality.

Building authentic confidence:

1. Prepare thoroughly: Knowledge is power. The more you know about the company, role, and your own experiences, the more confident you'll feel.
2. Practice positive self-talk: Replace negative thoughts with affirming ones. Instead of "I'm not qualified," think "I have unique skills to offer."
3. Visualize success: Spend time imagining yourself performing well in the interview.
4. Focus on your strengths: Make a list of your accomplishments and review them before the interview.
5. Adopt confident body language: Practice power poses before the interview to boost your confidence hormones.

The Likeability Factor

Research shows that likeability plays a significant role in hiring decisions. While qualifications are important, interviewers are also assessing whether you'd be a good fit for their team. This is where the concept of "affinity bias" comes into play—people tend to like those who are similar to them or who they can relate to.

Strategies to enhance your likeability:

1. Find common ground: Look for shared interests or experiences with your interviewer.
2. Show genuine interest: Ask thoughtful questions about the company and role.
3. Use appropriate humor: A well-timed light-hearted comment can build rapport.
4. Practice active listening: Show that you value the interviewer's input.
5. Mirror body language: Subtly match the interviewer's tone and posture to build unconscious rapport.

Managing Interview Anxiety

It's normal to feel nervous before and during an interview. However, excessive anxiety can impair your performance. Understanding the physiological aspects of anxiety and having strategies to manage it can make a significant difference.

Techniques for managing interview anxiety:

1. Controlled breathing: Practice deep, slow breathing to activate your

body's relaxation response.
2. Progressive muscle relaxation: Tense and relax different muscle groups to release physical tension.
3. Cognitive reframing: Change your perspective on the interview from a threat to a challenge or opportunity.
4. Preparation rituals: Develop a pre-interview routine that helps you feel centered and confident.
5. Mindfulness techniques: Use mindfulness to stay present and focused during the interview.

The Impression Management Game

Impression management is the conscious or subconscious process of attempting to influence others' perceptions. In an interview context, it's about presenting yourself in the best possible light while remaining authentic.

Key aspects of impression management:

1. Self-promotion: Highlighting your achievements and skills without appearing boastful.
2. Ingratiation: Building rapport and goodwill with the interviewer.
3. Exemplification: Demonstrating your work ethic and commitment.
4. Supplication: Showing a willingness to learn and grow (without undermining your competence).
5. Intimidation: Generally best avoided in interviews, but assertiveness can be appropriate in some contexts.

The Power of Authenticity

While impression management is important, authenticity should not be sacrificed. Interviewers can often sense when a candidate is being disingenuous. Moreover, pretending to be someone you're not is mentally taxing and can undermine your performance.

Balancing authenticity with strategic self-presentation:

1. Know your values and stay true to them.
2. Be honest about your experiences and skills.
3. Show vulnerability in appropriate ways (e.g., discussing a challenge you've overcome).
4. Let your personality shine through while maintaining professionalism.
5. If you don't know something, admit it, but express eagerness to learn.

The Reciprocity Principle

Psychologist Robert Cialdini identified reciprocity as a key principle of influence. In an interview context, this means that if you provide value to the interviewer (through insightful comments or questions), they're more likely to view you favorably.

Applying the reciprocity principle:

1. Offer unique insights about the industry or company.
2. Share ideas that could benefit the organization.
3. Provide thoughtful, well-researched responses that add value to the conversation.
4. Express genuine appreciation for the interviewer's time and insights.

The Halo Effect

CHAPTER 1: THE PSYCHOLOGY OF SUCCESSFUL INTERVIEWS: MINDSET...

The halo effect is a cognitive bias where one positive trait influences the overall impression of a person. In interviews, making a strong first impression can positively influence how the rest of your responses are perceived.

Leveraging the halo effect:

1. Nail your introduction and "tell me about yourself" response.
2. Dress appropriately and pay attention to grooming.
3. Start with your strongest examples and achievements.
4. Maintain positive energy throughout the interview.

Conclusion

Understanding the psychology of successful interviews empowers you to approach them with a winning mindset. By cultivating the right psychological approach—balancing confidence with authenticity, managing anxiety, and applying principles of social psychology—you set the stage for a stellar interview performance.

Remember, the most successful interviewees are those who not only showcase their skills and experience but also connect with interviewers on a human level. As you move forward in your interview preparation, keep these psychological principles in mind. They will serve as the foundation upon which you'll build your specific interview strategies and responses.

In the next chapter, we'll explore how to make a powerful first impression, building on the psychological groundwork we've laid here. Your mindset shapes your performance, and with the right psychological approach, you're already halfway to acing your interview.Chapter 1: The Psychology of Successful Interviews: Mindset Matters

The moment you step into an interview room, you're not just presenting your skills and experience—you're engaging in a complex psychological dance. Understanding the psychology behind successful interviews is the foundation upon which all other interview skills are built. In this chapter, we'll explore how your mindset can make or break your interview performance and provide you with strategies to cultivate a winning psychological approach.

The Power of Mindset

Carol Dweck, a renowned psychologist, introduced the concept of growth versus fixed mindsets. In the context of job interviews, adopting a growth mindset—the belief that your abilities can be developed through dedication and hard work—is crucial. This mindset allows you to view the interview as an opportunity for learning and growth, rather than a do-or-die test of your worth.

Cultivating a growth mindset for interviews involves:

1. Embracing challenges: See difficult questions as opportunities to showcase your problem-solving skills.
2. Persisting in the face of setbacks: If you stumble on a question, recover gracefully and move forward.
3. Viewing effort as the path to mastery: Recognize that thorough preparation is key to interview success.
4. Learning from criticism: Use feedback from past interviews to improve your performance.
5. Finding lessons and inspiration in others' success: Study successful interview strategies and adapt them to your style.

The Confidence Conundrum

CHAPTER 1: THE PSYCHOLOGY OF SUCCESSFUL INTERVIEWS: MINDSET...

Confidence is a critical factor in interview success, but it's a delicate balance. Too little confidence can make you appear unsure and incompetent, while overconfidence might come across as arrogance. The key is to project authentic confidence—a quiet assurance in your abilities that's grounded in reality.

Building authentic confidence:

1. Prepare thoroughly: Knowledge is power. The more you know about the company, role, and your own experiences, the more confident you'll feel.
2. Practice positive self-talk: Replace negative thoughts with affirming ones. Instead of "I'm not qualified," think "I have unique skills to offer."
3. Visualize success: Spend time imagining yourself performing well in the interview.
4. Focus on your strengths: Make a list of your accomplishments and review them before the interview.
5. Adopt confident body language: Practice power poses before the interview to boost your confidence hormones.

The Likeability Factor

Research shows that likeability plays a significant role in hiring decisions. While qualifications are important, interviewers are also assessing whether you'd be a good fit for their team. This is where the concept of "affinity bias" comes into play—people tend to like those who are similar to them or who they can relate to.

Strategies to enhance your likeability:

1. Find common ground: Look for shared interests or experiences with your interviewer.
2. Show genuine interest: Ask thoughtful questions about the company and role.
3. Use appropriate humor: A well-timed light-hearted comment can build rapport.
4. Practice active listening: Show that you value the interviewer's input.
5. Mirror body language: Subtly match the interviewer's tone and posture to build unconscious rapport.

Managing Interview Anxiety

It's normal to feel nervous before and during an interview. However, excessive anxiety can impair your performance. Understanding the physiological aspects of anxiety and having strategies to manage it can make a significant difference.

Techniques for managing interview anxiety:

1. Controlled breathing: Practice deep, slow breathing to activate your body's relaxation response.
2. Progressive muscle relaxation: Tense and relax different muscle groups to release physical tension.
3. Cognitive reframing: Change your perspective on the interview from a threat to a challenge or opportunity.
4. Preparation rituals: Develop a pre-interview routine that helps you feel centered and confident.
5. Mindfulness techniques: Use mindfulness to stay present and focused during the interview.

CHAPTER 1: THE PSYCHOLOGY OF SUCCESSFUL INTERVIEWS: MINDSET...

The Impression Management Game

Impression management is the conscious or subconscious process of attempting to influence others' perceptions. In an interview context, it's about presenting yourself in the best possible light while remaining authentic.

Key aspects of impression management:

1. Self-promotion: Highlighting your achievements and skills without appearing boastful.
2. Ingratiation: Building rapport and goodwill with the interviewer.
3. Exemplification: Demonstrating your work ethic and commitment.
4. Supplication: Showing a willingness to learn and grow (without undermining your competence).
5. Intimidation: Generally best avoided in interviews, but assertiveness can be appropriate in some contexts.

The Power of Authenticity

While impression management is important, authenticity should not be sacrificed. Interviewers can often sense when a candidate is being disingenuous. Moreover, pretending to be someone you're not is mentally taxing and can undermine your performance.

Balancing authenticity with strategic self-presentation:

1. Know your values and stay true to them.
2. Be honest about your experiences and skills.
3. Show vulnerability in appropriate ways (e.g., discussing a challenge you've overcome).

4. Let your personality shine through while maintaining professionalism.
5. If you don't know something, admit it, but express eagerness to learn.

The Reciprocity Principle

Psychologist Robert Cialdini identified reciprocity as a key principle of influence. In an interview context, this means that if you provide value to the interviewer (through insightful comments or questions), they're more likely to view you favorably.

Applying the reciprocity principle:

1. Offer unique insights about the industry or company.
2. Share ideas that could benefit the organization.
3. Provide thoughtful, well-researched responses that add value to the conversation.
4. Express genuine appreciation for the interviewer's time and insights.

The Halo Effect

The halo effect is a cognitive bias where one positive trait influences the overall impression of a person. In interviews, making a strong first impression can positively influence how the rest of your responses are perceived.

Leveraging the halo effect:

1. Nail your introduction and "tell me about yourself" response.
2. Dress appropriately and pay attention to grooming.

3. Start with your strongest examples and achievements.
4. Maintain positive energy throughout the interview.

Conclusion

Understanding the psychology of successful interviews empowers you to approach them with a winning mindset. By cultivating the right psychological approach—balancing confidence with authenticity, managing anxiety, and applying principles of social psychology—you set the stage for a stellar interview performance.

Remember, the most successful interviewees are those who not only showcase their skills and experience but also connect with interviewers on a human level. As you move forward in your interview preparation, keep these psychological principles in mind. They will serve as the foundation upon which you'll build your specific interview strategies and responses.

In the next chapter, we'll explore how to make a powerful first impression, building on the psychological groundwork we've laid here. Your mindset shapes your performance, and with the right psychological approach, you're already halfway to acing your interview.

Chapter 2: First Impressions: Dress, Body Language, and Etiquette

The old adage "you never get a second chance to make a first impression" holds particularly true in job interviews. Research suggests that interviewers form initial judgments about candidates within the first seven seconds of meeting them. These snap judgments can significantly influence the entire interview process. In this chapter, we'll explore how to make a powerful first impression through your dress, body language, and etiquette.

The Power of Appearance

Your appearance is the first thing an interviewer notices about you. It's not just about looking good; it's about demonstrating professionalism, attention to detail, and an understanding of the company culture.

Dressing for Success:

1. Research the company culture: Dress slightly more formally than the everyday office attire.
2. Choose well-fitting, clean, and pressed clothing: Ill-fitting or wrinkled clothes can suggest carelessness.
3. Opt for conservative colors: Navy, black, and gray are safe choices for

CHAPTER 2: FIRST IMPRESSIONS: DRESS, BODY LANGUAGE, AND...

  suits or dresses.
4. Pay attention to grooming: Ensure your hair is neat, nails are clean, and any facial hair is well-groomed.
5. Minimize distractions: Avoid overpowering fragrances, flashy jewelry, or loud patterns.
6. Shine your shoes: Well-maintained footwear indicates attention to detail.
7. Prepare your outfit the night before: This reduces stress on the day of the interview.

Remember, while you want to look professional, you also want to feel comfortable. Choose an outfit that makes you feel confident and allows you to focus on the interview rather than your clothes.

The Language of the Body

Your body language can speak volumes before you even say a word. Non-verbal cues can convey confidence, interest, and engagement – or the opposite if you're not careful.

Key aspects of positive body language:

1. Posture: Stand and sit up straight to project confidence and attentiveness.
2. Handshake: Offer a firm, dry handshake with eye contact and a smile.
3. Eye contact: Maintain consistent eye contact to show engagement, but don't stare.
4. Facial expressions: Keep a pleasant, interested expression. Smile naturally when appropriate.
5. Hand gestures: Use open hand gestures to appear honest and engaging. Avoid crossing your arms or fidgeting.

6. Mirroring: Subtly mirror the interviewer's body language to build rapport.
7. Leaning: Lean slightly forward to show interest, but respect personal space.

Practice these elements in front of a mirror or with a friend. Video recording yourself in a mock interview can also provide valuable insights into your non-verbal communication.

The Art of Interview Etiquette

Proper etiquette demonstrates respect for the interviewer and the process. It also shows that you understand professional norms and can navigate social situations skillfully.

Essential interview etiquette:

1. Punctuality: Arrive 10-15 minutes early. Being late is rarely excusable.
2. Greetings: Address the interviewer by their title and last name unless invited to do otherwise.
3. Small talk: Engage in light, professional small talk if the opportunity arises.
4. Electronics: Turn off your phone or put it on silent mode. Never check it during the interview.
5. Note-taking: Ask permission before taking notes during the interview.
6. Interruptions: Allow the interviewer to finish speaking before you respond.
7. Language: Use professional language and avoid slang or inappropriate humor.
8. Attitude: Show enthusiasm for the role and the company.
9. Closure: Thank the interviewer for their time at the end of the interview.

Remember, etiquette extends to everyone you encounter during your visit, from receptionists to potential future colleagues. Treat everyone with respect and courtesy.

Navigating the Digital First Impression

In the age of virtual interviews, making a strong first impression through a screen presents unique challenges and opportunities.

Tips for virtual interview impressions:

1. Test your technology: Ensure your camera, microphone, and internet connection are working well.
2. Choose an appropriate background: Select a clean, professional-looking space or use a neutral virtual background.
3. Lighting: Position yourself facing a light source to avoid appearing backlit or shadowed.
4. Camera angle: Position your camera at eye level for the most flattering and engaged appearance.
5. Dress fully: While it might be tempting to only dress professionally from the waist up, wearing complete professional attire can help you feel more prepared and avoid embarrassment if you need to stand up.
6. Make "eye contact" by looking at the camera: This helps create a connection with the interviewer.
7. Minimize distractions: Inform household members about your interview, silence notifications, and remove pets from the room.

The Importance of Authenticity

While focusing on making a positive first impression, it's crucial to remain authentic. Trying to present a completely different persona can come across as insincere and make you appear uncomfortable.

Balancing polish with authenticity:

1. Be yourself, but be your best professional self.
2. Let your personality shine through in appropriate ways.
3. If you make a mistake, handle it gracefully rather than trying to cover it up.
4. Use language that feels natural to you while maintaining professionalism.

Recovering from a Poor Start

Despite your best preparations, sometimes things don't go as planned. Perhaps you spill coffee on your shirt or trip on your way in. The key is to recover gracefully.

Strategies for bouncing back:

1. Address the issue directly but briefly.
2. Use humor if appropriate, but don't dwell on the mishap.
3. Refocus the attention on your qualifications and enthusiasm for the role.
4. Remember that how you handle adversity can itself make a positive impression.

Cultural Considerations

In our globalized world, it's important to be aware of cultural differences that might affect first impressions.

Cultural awareness tips:

1. Research cultural norms if interviewing in a different country or with a multinational company.
2. Be aware of differences in personal space, eye contact, and physical contact norms.
3. If unsure about a cultural practice, it's okay to politely ask for guidance.

The Lasting Impact of First Impressions

While a strong first impression sets a positive tone for the interview, it's important to maintain that positive image throughout your interaction. Consistency is key – your appearance, body language, and etiquette should align with your words and qualifications.

Remember that first impressions are not just about the first few seconds. They encompass your entire initial encounter, including:

1. Your interactions with reception staff
2. How you conduct yourself while waiting
3. Your behavior immediately after the interview concludes

Each of these moments contributes to the overall first impression you leave.

Conclusion

Making a strong first impression is both an art and a science. It requires careful preparation, self-awareness, and the ability to present your best professional self authentically. By paying attention to your dress, body language, and etiquette, you set the stage for a successful interview.

As you prepare for your next interview, take time to consider each aspect of your first impression. Practice your handshake, choose your outfit thoughtfully, and rehearse your initial greeting. Remember, confidence is key – and confidence comes from preparation.

In the next chapter, we'll delve into the crucial task of researching the company, which will not only help you answer questions more effectively but also inform how you present yourself from the moment you walk through the door. Your first impression should convey not just professionalism, but also genuine interest and fit with the organization – and that starts with thorough research.

Chapter 3: Researching the Company: Become an Insider Before You Walk In

In today's competitive job market, simply knowing the basics about a company is no longer enough to stand out in an interview. To truly impress your interviewers and demonstrate your genuine interest in the role, you need to become an "insider" before you even step through the door. This chapter will guide you through the process of conducting thorough, strategic research that will give you a significant edge in your interview.

Why In-Depth Research Matters

Comprehensive company research serves multiple purposes:

1. It demonstrates your genuine interest in the company and role.
2. It helps you align your skills and experiences with the company's needs.
3. It enables you to ask insightful questions during the interview.
4. It allows you to envision yourself in the role and speak confidently about your potential contributions.
5. It helps you determine if the company and role are truly a good fit for you.

The Basics: Where to Start

Begin with the company's official channels:

1. Company website: Thoroughly explore all sections, including About Us, Products/Services, Careers, and Press Releases.
2. Social media profiles: Follow the company on LinkedIn, Twitter, Facebook, and Instagram to get a sense of their public persona and recent activities.
3. Annual reports: For public companies, these provide valuable financial and strategic information.
4. Company blog: Often a source of insights into company culture and current projects.

Going Deeper: Advanced Research Techniques

To truly stand out, you need to go beyond the obvious sources:

1. Industry news and analysis:
   - Read industry-specific publications and websites.
   - Follow key industry influencers on social media.
   - Look for analyst reports on the company and its competitors.

2. Employee insights:
   - Check company reviews on sites like Glassdoor and Indeed.
   - Look for employee interviews or profiles on the company's website or in media coverage.
   - If possible, reach out to current or former employees for informational interviews.

3. Competitive landscape:
   - Identify the company's main competitors.
   - Analyze how the company positions itself in relation to these competitors.

CHAPTER 3: RESEARCHING THE COMPANY: BECOME AN INSIDER BEFORE...

- Look for recent news about market shifts or technological disruptions in the industry.

4. Company leadership:
   - Research the backgrounds of key executives and board members.
   - Look for interviews or articles featuring company leaders to understand their vision and management style.

5. Company culture and values:
   - Pay attention to how the company describes its culture and values.
   - Look for evidence of these values in action through company initiatives or employee testimonials.

6. Recent news and developments:
   - Set up Google Alerts for the company and its key products or services.
   - Check for recent press releases, product launches, or major announcements.

7. Financial health (for public companies):
   - Review recent quarterly reports and earnings calls transcripts.
   - Look for analyst opinions on the company's financial outlook.

8. Regulatory environment:
   - Understand any key regulations or legal issues affecting the company or industry.
   - Look for the company's stance on relevant policy issues.

9. Corporate social responsibility:
   - Research the company's sustainability initiatives and community involvement.
   - Look for evidence of ethical business practices and commitment to diversity and inclusion.

10. Future outlook:
   - Look for information about the company's long-term strategy and growth plans.
   - Consider how industry trends might impact the company's future.

Organizing Your Research

As you gather information, it's crucial to organize it in a way that's easily accessible during your interview preparation:

1. Create a document or spreadsheet with key information categorized (e.g., company history, recent news, key products, main competitors).
2. Develop a list of potential questions based on your research.
3. Identify specific points where your skills and experiences align with the company's needs or challenges.

Applying Your Research in the Interview

Your research should inform various aspects of your interview:

1. Tailoring your responses:
   - Use your knowledge of the company to customize your answers to common interview questions.
   - Demonstrate how your skills and experiences align with the company's specific needs and challenges.

2. Asking insightful questions:
   - Prepare thoughtful questions that show you've done your homework.
   - Ask about recent developments or future plans you've uncovered in your research.

CHAPTER 3: RESEARCHING THE COMPANY: BECOME AN INSIDER BEFORE...

3. Demonstrating cultural fit:
   - Reference aspects of the company culture that resonate with you.
   - Share examples of how you've thrived in similar environments.

4. Discussing industry trends:
   - Be prepared to share your thoughts on how current trends might impact the company.
   - Demonstrate your understanding of the broader context in which the company operates.

5. Addressing challenges:
   - If you've identified challenges the company is facing, be prepared to discuss how you might contribute to solutions.

6. Connecting with the interviewer:
   - If you know who will be interviewing you, research their background for potential common ground.
   - Reference relevant work or statements by company leaders if appropriate.

Avoiding Common Pitfalls

While thorough research is crucial, be mindful of these potential pitfalls:

1. Information overload: Focus on the most relevant and recent information.
2. Overreliance on unofficial sources: Be cautious about information from unverified sources or disgruntled former employees.
3. Appearing overly rehearsed: Use your research to inform your responses, but remain conversational and authentic.
4. Bringing up sensitive information: Be tactful about mentioning any negative press or controversies.

Continuous Learning

Remember that your research shouldn't stop once you walk into the interview. The business world is dynamic, and new developments can occur rapidly. Stay updated until the day of your interview, and be prepared to discuss any breaking news or recent announcements.

Conclusion

Becoming a company "insider" before your interview requires time, effort, and strategic thinking. However, the payoff is substantial. By conducting thorough research, you'll not only impress your interviewers with your knowledge and genuine interest, but you'll also be better equipped to determine if the company and role are truly the right fit for you.

As you move forward in your interview preparation, use the insights gained from your research to inform every aspect of your approach. In the next chapter, we'll explore how to craft your personal brand and align it with the company's needs and culture, building on the foundation of knowledge you've established through your research.

Remember, in today's competitive job market, being well-informed isn't just an advantage – it's a necessity. Your dedication to understanding the company in depth will set you apart and demonstrate the value you can bring to the organization from day one.

Chapter 4: Crafting Your Personal Brand: Aligning Your Story with the Job

In today's competitive job market, having the right skills and experience is just the starting point. To truly stand out and make a lasting impression, you need to craft a compelling personal brand that aligns seamlessly with the job you're pursuing. Your personal brand is the unique combination of skills, experiences, and personality that you want others to see. In this chapter, we'll explore how to develop and communicate your personal brand effectively, ensuring that it resonates with potential employers and positions you as the ideal candidate for the job.

Understanding Personal Branding

Personal branding is the practice of marketing yourself and your career as a brand. It's about creating a clear, consistent message about who you are professionally, what you excel at, and the unique value you bring to an organization. Your personal brand should:

1. Reflect your authentic self
2. Highlight your strengths and unique qualities
3. Be consistent across all professional platforms
4. Align with the needs and culture of your target employers

Identifying Your Unique Value Proposition

The first step in crafting your personal brand is to identify your Unique Value Proposition (UVP). This is the special combination of skills, experiences, and qualities that set you apart from other candidates. To determine your UVP:

1. List your key skills and strengths
2. Identify your most significant achievements
3. Consider feedback you've received from colleagues and supervisors
4. Reflect on what motivates you and what you're passionate about
5. Think about the problems you're best at solving

Once you've identified these elements, look for patterns and themes. What unique combination of traits emerges? This forms the core of your personal brand.

Aligning Your Brand with the Job

Now that you've identified your UVP, it's time to align it with the specific job you're pursuing. This involves:

1. Thoroughly analyzing the job description
2. Researching the company culture and values
3. Identifying the key challenges and objectives of the role
4. Understanding the broader industry context

With this information, you can tailor your personal brand to emphasize the aspects that are most relevant to the position. For example, if you're applying for a project management role in a fast-paced tech startup, you might

CHAPTER 4: CRAFTING YOUR PERSONAL BRAND: ALIGNING YOUR STORY...

emphasize your ability to lead agile teams, your track record of delivering projects under tight deadlines, and your passion for emerging technologies.

Crafting Your Brand Story

Your brand story is the narrative that brings your personal brand to life. It should be a compelling account of your professional journey, highlighting the experiences and insights that have shaped you into the ideal candidate for the job. When crafting your brand story:

1. Start with a hook: Begin with an engaging anecdote or statement that captures attention.
2. Highlight key milestones: Focus on the experiences that have been most formative in your career.
3. Emphasize growth and learning: Show how you've developed and adapted over time.
4. Incorporate your values: Demonstrate how your personal values align with those of the company.
5. Connect to the present: Explain how your past experiences have prepared you for this specific role.
6. Look to the future: Express your vision for what you hope to achieve in the position.

Remember, your brand story should be adaptable. While the core elements remain consistent, you should be able to emphasize different aspects depending on the specific job or company you're targeting.

Communicating Your Brand

Once you've defined your personal brand and crafted your story, you need to communicate it effectively across various platforms:

1. Resume: Ensure your resume reflects your brand by highlighting relevant achievements and using language that aligns with your brand identity.

2. LinkedIn Profile: Use your summary section to tell your brand story concisely. Ensure your experience section reinforces your brand messaging.

3. Cover Letter: Use this as an opportunity to expand on your brand story and explicitly connect it to the job requirements.

4. Portfolio or Personal Website: If relevant to your field, create a portfolio that showcases work aligned with your brand.

5. Elevator Pitch: Develop a concise, compelling summary of your brand that you can deliver in 30-60 seconds.

6. Interview Responses: Prepare anecdotes and examples that reinforce your brand message for common interview questions.

Demonstrating Brand Consistency

Consistency is key in personal branding. Ensure that your brand message is cohesive across all touchpoints:

1. Use consistent language and tone across all written materials
2. Ensure your online presence (social media, personal website) aligns with your professional brand
3. Dress and present yourself in a way that reflects your brand during interviews
4. Be mindful of your body language and communication style during in-person interactions

Avoiding Common Branding Pitfalls

As you develop your personal brand, be wary of these common mistakes:

1. Over-exaggeration: While it's important to highlight your strengths, don't make claims you can't back up.
2. Lack of authenticity: Your brand should be a true reflection of who you are, not who you think others want you to be.
3. Inflexibility: While consistency is important, be prepared to evolve your brand as your career progresses.
4. Neglecting online presence: In today's digital age, your online brand is often the first impression you make.
5. Focusing too much on yourself: Remember to always connect your brand back to how you can add value to the employer.

Evolving Your Brand

Your personal brand isn't static—it should evolve as you grow professionally. Regularly reassess your brand to ensure it still accurately reflects who you are and where you want to go in your career. Consider:

1. New skills or qualifications you've acquired
2. Significant achievements or experiences
3. Changes in your career goals or industry focus
4. Feedback from mentors, colleagues, or recruiters

Conclusion

Crafting a strong personal brand that aligns with your target job is a powerful way to set yourself apart in the job market. It requires self-reflection, strategic thinking, and consistent execution, but the rewards are significant. A well-crafted personal brand not only helps you make a strong impression in interviews but also guides your overall career development.

Remember, your personal brand is more than just a marketing tool for job interviews—it's a reflection of your professional identity and a roadmap for your career. By thoughtfully developing and consistently communicating your brand, you position yourself not just for success in your next interview, but for long-term career fulfillment.

As you move forward in your interview preparation, keep your personal brand at the forefront of your mind. In the next chapter, we'll explore how to tackle common interview questions, using your newly refined personal brand as a foundation for crafting compelling, authentic responses that showcase why you're the ideal candidate for the job.

Chapter 5: Mastering Common Interview Questions (and Dreaded Curveballs)

Preparing for common interview questions is essential, but truly mastering them—and being ready for unexpected curveballs—can set you apart as a standout candidate. This chapter will guide you through strategies for answering frequently asked questions, techniques for handling challenging or unexpected queries, and methods to ensure your responses align with your personal brand and the job requirements.

Common Interview Questions and Strategies

1. "Tell me about yourself."
This question often serves as an opener and sets the tone for the rest of the interview.
Strategy:
- Provide a concise summary of your professional journey
- Highlight key achievements relevant to the role
- Conclude with why you're interested in this position

Example structure: "I'm a marketing professional with 7 years of experience in digital advertising. In my current role at XYZ Corp, I've led campaigns that increased customer engagement by 40%. I'm particularly excited about this opportunity because…"

2. "Why do you want to work for our company?"

This question tests your knowledge of the company and your genuine interest.

Strategy:
- Demonstrate your research on the company
- Connect the company's mission or values to your own
- Explain how you can contribute to their goals

3. "What are your greatest strengths?"

Choose strengths that align with the job requirements.

Strategy:
- Provide 2-3 relevant strengths
- Give concrete examples of how you've demonstrated these strengths
- Explain how these strengths will benefit the company

4. "What is your greatest weakness?"

This question assesses your self-awareness and ability to improve.

Strategy:
- Choose a genuine weakness that isn't critical to the job
- Explain steps you're taking to improve
- If possible, show how you've already made progress

Example: "I used to struggle with public speaking. To address this, I joined Toastmasters and have been practicing regularly. Recently, I successfully presented to a group of 50 clients."

5. "Where do you see yourself in five years?"

This question gauges your ambition and commitment.

Strategy:
- Show alignment between your career goals and potential growth within the company
- Demonstrate your commitment to continuous learning
- Express enthusiasm for growing with the organization

CHAPTER 5: MASTERING COMMON INTERVIEW QUESTIONS (AND DREADED...

6. "Can you describe a challenging work situation and how you overcame it?"

This behavioral question assesses your problem-solving skills and resilience.

Strategy:
- Use the STAR method (Situation, Task, Action, Result)
- Choose a relevant example that highlights your skills
- Focus on positive outcomes and lessons learned

7. "Why should we hire you?"

This is your opportunity to summarize your value proposition.

Strategy:
- Align your skills and experience with the job requirements
- Highlight your unique strengths and achievements
- Express enthusiasm for contributing to the company's success

Handling Curveball Questions

Interviewers sometimes throw unexpected questions to assess how you think on your feet. Here are strategies for handling curveballs:

1. Take a moment to think

It's okay to pause briefly to gather your thoughts. A thoughtful response is better than a rushed one.

2. Ask for clarification if needed

If you're unsure about the question, it's perfectly acceptable to ask for clarification.

3. Stay calm and positive

Even if the question catches you off guard, maintain your composure and a positive attitude.

4. Draw from your preparation

Often, you can adapt answers from your preparation for common questions to address unexpected ones.

5. Be honest if you don't know

If you genuinely don't know the answer, it's better to admit it and explain how you'd find the information.

Examples of curveball questions and how to handle them:

1. "If you were an animal, what would you be and why?"

Purpose: To assess creativity and self-awareness.

Strategy: Choose an animal with positive qualities that align with the job requirements.

Example: "I'd be a dolphin because they're known for their intelligence, teamwork, and adaptability—qualities I strive to bring to my work."

2. "How many golf balls can fit in a school bus?"

Purpose: To evaluate your problem-solving approach.

Strategy: Think out loud, break down the problem, and explain your reasoning.

Example: "To answer this, I'd need to know the volume of a golf ball and a school bus. Let's estimate…"

3. "What would your previous boss say is your greatest weakness?"

Purpose: To gauge your self-awareness and honesty.

Strategy: Be honest but strategic. Choose a weakness your boss might mention that you've actively worked to improve.

4. "Sell me this pen."

Purpose: To assess your sales and communication skills.

Strategy: Ask questions to understand the "buyer's" needs, then highlight the pen's features that address those needs.

CHAPTER 5: MASTERING COMMON INTERVIEW QUESTIONS (AND DREADED...

5. "How would you explain our product to a 5-year-old?"
Purpose: To evaluate your ability to simplify complex concepts.
Strategy: Use simple language and relatable analogies.

Techniques for Effective Answering

1. Use the STAR method for behavioral questions
   Situation: Set the context
   Task: Explain your responsibility
   Action: Describe what you did
   Result: Share the outcome and lessons learned

2. Quantify your achievements
   Use specific numbers and percentages to make your accomplishments more impactful.

3. Tailor your answers to the job
   Always connect your responses back to the requirements of the position.

4. Be concise
   Aim for responses that are 1-2 minutes long. If more detail is needed, the interviewer will ask.

5. Practice active listening
   Ensure you fully understand the question before answering. This helps avoid misunderstandings and allows for more targeted responses.

6. Use positive language
   Frame challenges as learning opportunities and focus on solutions rather than problems.

7. Prepare anecdotes
   Have a set of versatile stories ready that showcase your skills and can be

adapted to different questions.

8. Mirror the interviewer's style
Adapt your communication style to match the interviewer's pace and tone for better rapport.

Handling Difficult Questions

1. About employment gaps
Be honest and focus on what you learned or accomplished during that time.

2. About being overqualified
Emphasize your enthusiasm for the role and how your experience can benefit the company.

3. About salary expectations
Research industry standards and provide a range rather than a specific number.

4. About reasons for leaving previous jobs
Focus on what you're looking for in a new role rather than negative aspects of previous positions.

5. About conflicts with previous coworkers
Emphasize your problem-solving skills and the positive resolution of the conflict.

Conclusion

Mastering common interview questions and preparing for curveballs is about more than memorizing answers—it's about developing a flexible, strategic approach to showcasing your value as a candidate. By thoroughly preparing,

CHAPTER 5: MASTERING COMMON INTERVIEW QUESTIONS (AND DREADED...

practicing your responses, and staying adaptable, you'll be ready to handle whatever questions come your way with confidence and poise.

Remember, the key is to always bring your answers back to how you can add value to the company and the specific role. Use each question as an opportunity to reinforce your personal brand and demonstrate why you're the ideal candidate for the position.

In the next chapter, we'll delve into the STAR method in more detail, providing you with a powerful framework for structuring compelling responses to behavioral interview questions.

Chapter 6: The STAR Method: Structuring Compelling Responses

The STAR method is a powerful technique for structuring your responses to behavioral interview questions. These questions typically ask you to describe a specific situation from your past experience, and they often begin with phrases like "Tell me about a time when…" or "Describe a situation where…". The STAR method provides a framework that ensures your answers are comprehensive, concise, and compelling.

Understanding the STAR Method

STAR is an acronym that stands for:

Situation: Set the context for your story.
Task: Explain the challenge or responsibility you faced.
Action: Describe the specific actions you took to address the situation.
Result: Share the outcomes of your actions and what you learned.

Let's break down each component in detail:

Situation

This is where you set the stage for your story. Provide enough context for

CHAPTER 6: THE STAR METHOD: STRUCTURING COMPELLING RESPONSES

the interviewer to understand the circumstances, but keep it concise.

Key points:
- Briefly describe the setting (workplace, project, etc.)
- Mention when this occurred (if relevant)
- Explain any necessary background information

Example: "In my previous role as a marketing manager at XYZ Company, we were launching a new product line aimed at millennials. Our initial market research indicated low brand awareness among this demographic."

Task

Here, you outline the specific challenge or responsibility you faced in this situation.

Key points:
- Clearly state what was required of you
- Explain any constraints or difficulties you faced
- Highlight why this task was important

Example: "My task was to develop and implement a social media campaign that would increase brand awareness by 30% among millennials within three months, while staying within our limited budget of $50,000."

Action

This is the most crucial part of your response. Detail the specific steps you took to address the situation.

Key points:
- Focus on your individual actions (use "I" instead of "we")
- Be specific about the steps you took

- Explain your rationale for choosing these actions
- Highlight any skills or qualities you demonstrated

Example: "I began by conducting a thorough analysis of our target audience's social media habits. Based on this research, I identified Instagram and TikTok as our primary platforms. I then developed a content strategy that focused on user-generated content and influencer partnerships. I personally reached out to 20 micro-influencers in our niche, negotiating collaboration deals that fit our budget. Additionally, I created a hashtag challenge that encouraged users to showcase our products in creative ways."

Result

Conclude your response by sharing the outcomes of your actions. Where possible, quantify your results.

Key points:
- Provide specific, measurable results
- Explain how your actions contributed to these outcomes
- Share any lessons learned or skills gained
- If the outcome wasn't entirely positive, explain what you learned and how you'd approach it differently now

Example: "As a result of this campaign, we saw a 45% increase in brand awareness among millennials, exceeding our initial goal of 30%. Our Instagram followers grew by 10,000, and the hashtag challenge generated over 50,000 user submissions. This campaign not only achieved its primary objective but also resulted in a 20% increase in sales of the new product line. I learned the value of thorough audience research and the power of user-generated content in engaging younger demographics."

Implementing the STAR Method Effectively

CHAPTER 6: THE STAR METHOD: STRUCTURING COMPELLING RESPONSES

1. Prepare a variety of STAR stories

Before your interview, prepare several STAR stories that showcase different skills and experiences relevant to the job you're applying for. Having a range of examples ready will help you respond confidently to various behavioral questions.

2. Keep it relevant

Choose stories that are directly related to the job requirements. Review the job description and company information to identify key skills and qualities they're looking for, and prepare STAR examples that demonstrate these.

3. Be specific

Avoid generalities. Use concrete details and, where possible, quantifiable results to make your story more impactful and believable.

4. Practice, but don't memorize

While it's important to practice your STAR responses, avoid memorizing them word-for-word. This can make your answers sound rehearsed and unnatural. Instead, focus on remembering the key points of each story.

5. Keep it concise

Aim to keep your STAR responses to about 2-3 minutes. Practice trimming unnecessary details while ensuring you cover all four components.

6. Show growth

When possible, include what you learned from the experience or how you've applied these lessons in subsequent situations.

7. Be honest

While it's important to present yourself in the best light, never fabricate or exaggerate your stories. Experienced interviewers can often detect insincerity.

Common Pitfalls to Avoid

1. Focusing too much on the Situation and Task
   While context is important, the Action and Result components should be the meat of your response. They demonstrate your skills and the value you can bring to the company.

2. Not having a clear result
   Always include a clear, preferably quantifiable result. If the outcome wasn't positive, focus on what you learned and how you've applied this learning since.

3. Using the same example for multiple questions
   While it's okay to reference the same situation for different questions, vary your examples to showcase a range of skills and experiences.

4. Failing to connect your story to the job
   Always tie your STAR response back to the requirements of the position you're applying for.

5. Downplaying your role
   Even if it was a team effort, focus on your specific contributions and leadership in your STAR responses.

Adapting STAR for Different Types of Questions

While STAR is primarily used for behavioral questions, you can adapt this method for other types of interview questions:

1. Hypothetical questions
   For "What would you do if…" questions, use the STAR method to describe a similar situation you've faced in the past, then explain how you'd apply those lessons to the hypothetical scenario.

CHAPTER 6: THE STAR METHOD: STRUCTURING COMPELLING RESPONSES

2. Weakness questions

When asked about a weakness, use STAR to describe a time when you recognized and addressed a personal weakness, focusing on the positive outcome and growth.

3. Conflict resolution questions

Use STAR to describe a specific conflict, detailing the actions you took to resolve it and the positive result of your intervention.

Conclusion

The STAR method is a powerful tool for crafting compelling, structured responses to behavioral interview questions. By mastering this technique, you'll be able to confidently showcase your skills and experiences in a way that clearly demonstrates your value to potential employers.

Remember, the key to success with the STAR method is preparation and practice. Develop a repertoire of relevant stories, practice articulating them clearly and concisely, and be ready to adapt them to various questions. With these skills, you'll be well-equipped to impress interviewers and stand out as a top candidate.

In the next chapter, we'll explore how to showcase your achievements effectively, building on the STAR method to quantify your successes and make a lasting impression.

Chapter 7: Showcasing Your Achievements: Quantify Your Success

In the competitive landscape of job interviews, effectively showcasing your achievements can be the difference between landing your dream job and being passed over. While the STAR method provides a solid framework for structuring your responses, quantifying your success takes your answers to the next level. This chapter will explore how to identify, articulate, and present your achievements in a way that clearly demonstrates your value to potential employers.

The Power of Quantification

Quantifying your achievements serves several crucial purposes:

1. It provides concrete evidence of your capabilities
2. It helps interviewers understand the scale and impact of your work
3. It makes your accomplishments more memorable
4. It demonstrates your results-oriented mindset

Identifying Your Achievements

Before you can quantify your success, you need to identify your key achievements. Consider the following areas:

1. Performance metrics: Sales figures, productivity improvements, cost savings
2. Project outcomes: Timelines met, budgets managed, goals achieved
3. Team leadership: Size of teams led, improvements in team performance
4. Innovation: New processes implemented, problems solved
5. Customer satisfaction: Improved ratings, positive feedback received
6. Awards and recognition: Industry accolades, internal company awards

When identifying achievements, focus on those most relevant to the job you're applying for. Review the job description and company information to understand what kind of accomplishments would be most valued.

Quantifying Your Achievements

Once you've identified your key achievements, it's time to quantify them. Here are some strategies:

1. Use percentages
Percentages are powerful because they provide context and are easy to understand.
Example: "Increased customer retention rate by 25% over six months"

2. Provide actual numbers
When appropriate, use specific figures to illustrate the scale of your achievement.
Example: "Managed a team of 15 developers across 3 international offices"

3. Use time frames
Including time frames adds credibility and helps the interviewer under-

stand the pace of your accomplishments.

Example: "Implemented a new CRM system in just 3 months, 2 weeks ahead of schedule"

4. Compare "before and after" scenarios

This method clearly illustrates the impact of your actions.

Example: "Reduced average customer response time from 24 hours to 4 hours"

5. Mention scale

If you've worked on large-scale projects or with big clients, mentioning this can be impressive.

Example: "Led the product launch for our company's biggest client, a Fortune 500 tech firm"

6. Use industry benchmarks

If available, compare your achievements to industry standards.

Example: "Achieved a customer satisfaction score of 98%, 20 points above the industry average"

Presenting Your Quantified Achievements

Now that you've identified and quantified your achievements, it's crucial to present them effectively in your interview. Here are some tips:

1. Integrate them into your STAR responses

Use your quantified achievements as the "Result" in your STAR method responses.

Example: "As a result of the social media campaign I designed, we saw a 45% increase in engagement and a 30% boost in sales within the first quarter."

2. Prepare a "greatest hits" list

Have a mental list of your top 5-7 quantified achievements ready to weave into various interview questions.

3. Use visual aids when appropriate

If you're in a field where visual representation is valued (like design or data analysis), consider bringing a portfolio or presentation that visually showcases your quantified achievements.

4. Tailor to the job requirements

Emphasize the achievements most relevant to the position you're applying for.

5. Provide context

While numbers are powerful, make sure to explain why these achievements were significant in your role or for your company.

6. Be prepared to elaborate

Have additional details ready in case the interviewer asks for more information about a particular achievement.

Addressing Challenges in Quantification

Not all roles or achievements are easily quantifiable. Here are some strategies for dealing with common challenges:

1. Qualitative achievements

For roles where success is more qualitative, look for ways to indirectly quantify your impact.

Example: Instead of "Improved team morale," try "Implemented weekly team-building activities, resulting in a 30% decrease in employee turnover."

2. Collaborative achievements

When your achievement was part of a team effort, focus on your specific contributions and their impact on the overall result.

Example: "As the lead designer in a team of five, I was responsible for the UI overhaul that contributed to a 40% increase in user engagement."

3. Confidential information

If you can't disclose specific numbers due to confidentiality, use percentages or relative terms.

Example: Instead of specific revenue figures, say "Increased department revenue by 35% year-over-year."

4. New or evolving roles

In positions where you've built something from scratch, focus on growth metrics or comparisons to initial states.

Example: "Grew our social media following from zero to 100,000 in 18 months."

5. Long-term impact

For achievements where the full impact may not be immediately apparent, focus on interim metrics or projections.

Example: "Implemented a new training program projected to save the company $500,000 annually in reduced turnover costs."

Common Pitfalls to Avoid

1. Exaggeration

While it's important to present your achievements in the best light, avoid exaggerating or inflating your numbers. Experienced interviewers can often detect inconsistencies.

2. Focusing solely on numbers

While quantification is powerful, make sure to provide context and explain the significance of your achievements.

3. Neglecting soft skills

Don't forget to highlight achievements related to soft skills like communication, leadership, or problem-solving, even if they're harder to quantify.

4. Using jargon or technical terms
Ensure your achievements are understandable to someone outside your specific role or industry.

5. Taking full credit for team achievements
Be honest about your role in collaborative efforts while still highlighting your contributions.

Practicing Your Delivery

Once you've prepared your quantified achievements, practice incorporating them into your interview responses:

1. Role-play with a friend or mentor
Have them ask you common interview questions and practice weaving in your achievements.

2. Record yourself
Listen to how you present your achievements and refine your delivery.

3. Time your responses
Ensure you can present your achievements concisely within the context of longer responses.

4. Prepare for follow-up questions
Be ready to provide more details or explain the context of your achievements if asked.

Conclusion

Quantifying your achievements is a powerful way to make your interview responses more impactful and memorable. By providing concrete, measurable evidence of your successes, you demonstrate your value to potential employers in a clear and compelling manner. Remember, the goal is not just to impress with numbers, but to tell the story of your professional growth and the tangible impact you've had in your roles.

As you prepare for your interview, take the time to identify, quantify, and practice presenting your key achievements. This preparation will not only boost your confidence but also provide you with a arsenal of powerful examples to draw from during your interview.

In the next chapter, we'll explore how to address employment gaps and career transitions effectively, ensuring that you can present a cohesive and positive narrative of your professional journey.

Chapter 8: Addressing Employment Gaps and Career Transitions

In an ideal world, every professional would have a linear career path with no interruptions. However, the reality is often different. Employment gaps and career transitions are common experiences in today's dynamic job market. While these situations can be challenging to explain in an interview, with the right approach, you can turn them into opportunities to showcase your adaptability, growth, and diverse skill set.

Understanding Employment Gaps

Employment gaps are periods in your professional history where you were not formally employed. These can occur for various reasons, including:

1. Layoffs or company closures
2. Personal health issues
3. Caring for family members
4. Pursuing further education
5. Travel or personal growth experiences
6. Volunteering or unpaid work
7. Starting a business that didn't succeed

Regardless of the reason, it's crucial to approach employment gaps with honesty and a positive attitude.

Strategies for Addressing Employment Gaps

1. Be honest and concise
   Provide a brief, truthful explanation for your employment gap without oversharing personal details.

Example: "I took a year off to care for an ill family member. They've since recovered, and I'm excited to re-enter the workforce with renewed energy and perspective."

2. Focus on what you learned or accomplished
   Highlight any skills you developed or experiences you gained during your time away from formal employment.

Example: "During my six-month travel break, I immersed myself in different cultures and learned two new languages, which I believe will be valuable in this global marketing role."

3. Demonstrate how you stayed current
   Explain how you kept your skills sharp and stayed connected to your industry during your time away.

Example: "While taking time off to raise my children, I consistently followed industry trends through online courses and webinars, ensuring my skills remained up-to-date."

4. Show how the gap has made you a stronger candidate
   Frame your experience in a way that demonstrates personal growth and renewed motivation.

CHAPTER 8: ADDRESSING EMPLOYMENT GAPS AND CAREER TRANSITIONS

Example: "My experience starting my own business, though ultimately not successful, taught me valuable lessons about entrepreneurship and resilience that I'm eager to apply in a corporate setting."

5. Be prepared for follow-up questions

Have more detailed explanations ready in case the interviewer asks for additional information.

Navigating Career Transitions

Career transitions involve moving from one type of job or industry to another. These can be challenging to explain, but they also offer an opportunity to showcase your adaptability and diverse skill set.

Types of Career Transitions

1. Industry change (e.g., finance to technology)
2. Function change (e.g., marketing to human resources)
3. Level change (e.g., individual contributor to manager)
4. Work style change (e.g., corporate job to freelancing)

Strategies for Explaining Career Transitions

1. Highlight transferable skills

Identify and emphasize the skills from your previous career that are relevant to the new role.

Example: "While my background is in finance, the analytical and problem-solving skills I developed are directly applicable to data science, which is why I'm excited about this transition."

2. Explain your motivation

Clearly articulate why you're making the change and how it aligns with your long-term career goals.

Example: "After ten years in sales, I realized my true passion lies in developing the strategies behind the products. That's why I'm eager to transition into product management."

3. Demonstrate your commitment

Show how you've prepared for this transition through education, training, or side projects.

Example: "To prepare for this move into UX design, I've completed a comprehensive UX certification program and redesigned websites for three local non-profits."

4. Connect your past experience to the new role

Draw parallels between your previous work and the requirements of the new position.

Example: "My experience managing complex projects in construction has honed my organizational and leadership skills, which I believe will translate well to a project management role in software development."

5. Show enthusiasm and a willingness to learn

Express your excitement about the new field and your commitment to quickly getting up to speed.

Example: "I'm thrilled about the opportunity to apply my customer service skills in a new context. I'm a quick learner and am committed to rapidly developing my technical knowledge to excel in this IT support role."

Addressing Both Gaps and Transitions

CHAPTER 8: ADDRESSING EMPLOYMENT GAPS AND CAREER TRANSITIONS

Sometimes, an employment gap may coincide with a career transition. In these cases, it's important to craft a narrative that logically connects these experiences.

Example: "During my year off to travel, I discovered a passion for environmental conservation. This led me to volunteer with several eco-friendly organizations, where I developed new skills in sustainability practices. These experiences inspired my decision to transition from finance to a career in environmental consulting."

Preparing Your Narrative

When addressing gaps or transitions, preparation is key. Follow these steps:

1. Reflect on your experiences
   Take time to understand how your gap or transition has contributed to your professional growth.

2. Identify the positives
   List the skills, experiences, or perspectives you've gained that are relevant to the new role.

3. Craft your story
   Develop a clear, concise narrative that explains your gap or transition positively and professionally.

4. Practice your delivery
   Rehearse your explanation to ensure you can deliver it confidently and naturally.

5. Be consistent
   Ensure your explanation aligns with the information on your resume and LinkedIn profile.

Handling Difficult Questions

Interviewers may ask challenging questions about your gap or transition. Here are some examples and how to handle them:

Q: "Why were you out of work for so long?"
   A: "After being laid off, I took some time to reflect on my career goals and enhance my skills. I completed an advanced certification in [relevant area], which I believe makes me a stronger candidate for this role."

Q: "Why are you changing careers at this stage?"
   A: "While I've enjoyed my career in [previous field], I've realized that my true passion and strengths align more closely with [new field]. I'm excited about the opportunity to bring my unique perspective and transferable skills to this new challenge."

Q: "How do we know you're committed to this new field?"
   A: "I understand your concern. My decision to change fields wasn't made lightly. I've invested significant time in [relevant courses/certifications/projects] to prepare for this transition, and I'm committed to continuing my learning on the job."

Turning Negatives into Positives

Remember, employment gaps and career transitions are not inherently negative. They can demonstrate:

1. Adaptability and resilience
2. Self-awareness and the courage to make changes
3. Diverse experiences and perspectives
4. Commitment to personal and professional growth
5. The ability to handle challenges and uncertainty

CHAPTER 8: ADDRESSING EMPLOYMENT GAPS AND CAREER TRANSITIONS

Conclusion

Addressing employment gaps and career transitions effectively requires honesty, preparation, and a positive attitude. By framing these experiences as opportunities for growth and learning, you can turn potential red flags into compelling parts of your professional story.

Remember, many successful professionals have navigated gaps and transitions in their careers. The key is to show how these experiences have made you a stronger, more well-rounded candidate. With thoughtful preparation and confident delivery, you can address these aspects of your career history in a way that enhances, rather than detracts from, your candidacy.

In the next chapter, we'll explore the art of asking questions in an interview, another crucial aspect of showcasing your enthusiasm and fit for the role.

Chapter 9: The Art of Asking Questions: Impress with Your Curiosity

Asking thoughtful, insightful questions during a job interview is not just an opportunity—it's a crucial part of the interview process. It demonstrates your genuine interest in the role, showcases your preparation, and helps you gather valuable information to make an informed decision about the position. In this chapter, we'll explore the art of asking questions that will impress your interviewer and give you a competitive edge.

The Importance of Asking Questions

1. Shows your interest and enthusiasm for the role and company
2. Demonstrates that you've done your research
3. Helps you assess if the job and company are a good fit for you
4. Provides an opportunity to address any concerns or doubts you may have
5. Allows you to showcase your knowledge and critical thinking skills
6. Helps you stand out from other candidates

Preparing Your Questions

To ask impactful questions, thorough preparation is key:

CHAPTER 9: THE ART OF ASKING QUESTIONS: IMPRESS WITH YOUR...

1. Research the company: Study the company's website, recent news, annual reports, and social media presence.

2. Understand the role: Analyze the job description and think about how it fits into the larger organization.

3. Review your own goals: Consider what you want to know to determine if this role aligns with your career aspirations.

4. Prepare more questions than you'll need: Aim for 8-10 questions, as some may be answered during the course of the interview.

Types of Questions to Ask

1. Role-specific questions
   These questions show your interest in the day-to-day responsibilities and expectations of the position.

Examples:
   - "What does a typical day look like in this role?"
   - "What are the biggest challenges someone in this position would face?"
   - "How does this role contribute to the larger goals of the department/company?"

2. Company culture questions
   These help you understand the work environment and whether you'd be a good fit.

Examples:
   - "How would you describe the company's culture?"
   - "What types of employees tend to thrive here?"
   - "How does the company support work-life balance?"

3. Growth and development questions

These demonstrate your ambition and desire for long-term commitment.

Examples:
- "What opportunities for professional development does the company offer?"
- "How does the company support employee growth and advancement?"
- "Can you share an example of someone who has grown their career within the company?"

4. Team dynamics questions

These show your interest in how you'll fit into the existing team structure.

Examples:
- "Can you tell me about the team I'd be working with?"
- "How does this team collaborate with other departments?"
- "What's the management style of the person I'd be reporting to?"

5. Company direction questions

These questions showcase your strategic thinking and long-term perspective.

Examples:
- "What are the company's main goals for the next 3-5 years?"
- "How is the company adapting to [relevant industry trend]?"
- "What do you see as the biggest opportunities and challenges for the company in the near future?"

6. Performance measurement questions

These demonstrate your results-oriented mindset.

Examples:
- "How is success measured in this role?"

- "What KPIs would I be responsible for in this position?"
- "How often are performance reviews conducted?"

7. Next steps questions
These show your enthusiasm and proactivity.

Examples:
- "What are the next steps in the interview process?"
- "Is there any additional information I can provide to support my application?"

Strategies for Asking Effective Questions

1. Listen actively throughout the interview
Pay close attention to what's been said to avoid asking questions that have already been answered.

2. Ask open-ended questions
These encourage detailed responses and can lead to more insightful conversations.

3. Use the interviewer's responses to ask follow-up questions
This shows you're actively listening and can think on your feet.

4. Avoid yes/no questions
These typically lead to short answers and don't provide much valuable information.

5. Don't ask about salary or benefits in the first interview
Save these questions for later in the process, once you've established mutual interest.

6. Spread your questions throughout the interview

Don't save all your questions for the end. If appropriate, ask questions as relevant topics come up during the conversation.

7. Be mindful of time

Respect the interviewer's schedule. If time is running short, ask which of your remaining questions is most important to address.

Questions to Avoid

1. Basic information about the company

Asking questions that can be easily answered by the company's website shows a lack of preparation.

2. Personal questions about the interviewer

Unless directly relevant to the role, avoid overly personal queries.

3. Controversial topics

Steer clear of questions about politics, religion, or other sensitive subjects.

4. Negative questions about the company

Avoid questions that could be perceived as criticism of the company or its practices.

5. Questions about time off or work hours

While work-life balance is important, these questions can give the impression that you're more focused on time off than the job itself.

Turning the Tables: When the Interviewer Asks "Do You Have Any Questions?"

This common end-of-interview question is not just a formality—it's an opportunity. Here's how to handle it:

CHAPTER 9: THE ART OF ASKING QUESTIONS: IMPRESS WITH YOUR...

1. Always have questions ready
   Responding with "No, I think you've covered everything" can signal a lack of interest or preparation.

2. Choose questions strategically
   Select 2-3 of your most thought-provoking questions that haven't been addressed.

3. Use this as an opportunity to reinforce your interest
   Preface your questions with a statement of enthusiasm for the role.

Example: "Yes, I do have a few questions. First, I want to say that I'm very excited about this opportunity. One thing I'm particularly curious about is…"

4. Be prepared to ask a question about something discussed earlier
   This shows you were actively listening throughout the interview.

Making the Most of the Answers

Asking great questions is only half the equation. How you handle the responses is equally important:

1. Listen attentively
   Show genuine interest in the answers you receive.

2. Take notes
   This demonstrates your engagement and helps you remember key points.

3. Respond thoughtfully
   When appropriate, share brief insights or experiences related to the interviewer's response.

4. Use the information

Incorporate what you learn into your thank-you note or subsequent interviews.

Conclusion

The questions you ask in an interview are a powerful tool for demonstrating your interest, insight, and fit for the role. They're also your opportunity to gather the information you need to make an informed decision about the position.

Remember, an interview is a two-way street. While the company is assessing your suitability for the role, you're also evaluating whether the company and position align with your career goals and values. Thoughtful questions help you make this assessment while simultaneously impressing your interviewer with your curiosity and preparation.

As you prepare for your next interview, invest time in crafting insightful questions. Your ability to ask intelligent, relevant questions can set you apart from other candidates and leave a lasting positive impression on your potential employer.

In the next chapter, we'll explore how to navigate different interview formats, including one-on-one, panel, and group interviews, ensuring you're prepared for any interview scenario you might encounter.

Chapter 10: Navigating Different Interview Formats: One-on-One, Panel, and Group

In today's diverse job market, candidates must be prepared to face various interview formats. Each type of interview presents unique challenges and opportunities. Understanding how to navigate one-on-one, panel, and group interviews will boost your confidence and increase your chances of success. This chapter will explore strategies for excelling in each of these interview formats.

One-on-One Interviews

The one-on-one interview is the most common format. It typically involves a conversation between you and a single interviewer, often a hiring manager or HR representative.

Advantages:
 - More personal interaction
 - Easier to build rapport
 - Opportunity for in-depth discussion

Strategies for Success:

1. Focus on building a connection

Use the intimate setting to establish a personal connection with the interviewer. Maintain eye contact, use the interviewer's name, and look for common ground.

2. Pay attention to non-verbal cues
In a one-on-one setting, body language becomes more important. Be aware of your posture, facial expressions, and gestures.

3. Ask thoughtful questions
Use this format to ask more detailed questions about the role and company. The one-on-one setting allows for a more conversational approach.

4. Be prepared for silence
Some interviewers use silence as a tactic to see how you react. Stay calm and use these moments to gather your thoughts.

5. Adapt to the interviewer's style
Pay attention to whether the interviewer is more formal or casual, and try to match their tone appropriately.

Panel Interviews

Panel interviews involve multiple interviewers, typically representatives from different departments or levels within the organization.

Advantages:
    - Efficient for the company
    - Provides diverse perspectives on the candidate
    - Allows you to showcase how you interact with different personalities

Strategies for Success:

1. Research the panel members

CHAPTER 10: NAVIGATING DIFFERENT INTERVIEW FORMATS:...

If possible, find out who will be on the panel and research their roles. This will help you tailor your responses and questions.

2. Make eye contact with everyone
When answering a question, make eye contact with the person who asked it, but also engage other panel members.

3. Remember names and roles
Try to remember each panel member's name and position. Use their names when addressing them directly.

4. Be prepared for rapid-fire questions
Panel interviews can sometimes feel like a barrage of questions. Stay calm and take a moment to collect your thoughts if needed.

5. Bring extra copies of your resume
Ensure each panel member has a copy of your resume for reference.

6. Look for allies
Often, one or two panel members will be more responsive or friendly. While engaging with everyone, you can use these allies to boost your confidence.

7. Be consistent
Different panel members may ask similar questions. Ensure your answers remain consistent throughout the interview.

Group Interviews

Group interviews involve multiple candidates interviewing simultaneously. They may include group discussions, problem-solving exercises, or individual questions in a group setting.

Advantages:
   - Allows companies to see how candidates interact with others
   - Provides insight into leadership and teamwork skills
   - Efficient for initial screening of multiple candidates

Strategies for Success:

1. Stand out without dominating
   Contribute meaningfully to discussions, but avoid overshadowing others. Show leadership by encouraging quieter members to share their thoughts.

2. Listen actively
   Pay attention to what others are saying. Build on their ideas to demonstrate your collaboration skills.

3. Be aware of your body language
   In a group setting, your non-verbal communication is always on display. Maintain an engaged and positive demeanor throughout.

4. Prepare a strong self-introduction
   You may be asked to introduce yourself to the group. Prepare a concise, impactful introduction that highlights your key strengths.

5. Show respect for others
   Demonstrate your interpersonal skills by being courteous to both the interviewers and other candidates.

6. Be prepared for impromptu tasks
   Group interviews often include unexpected exercises. Stay calm and approach these tasks with enthusiasm.

7. Remember it's not a competition
   While you want to stand out, avoid directly competing with other candi-

CHAPTER 10: NAVIGATING DIFFERENT INTERVIEW FORMATS:...

dates. Focus on showcasing your own strengths rather than highlighting others' weaknesses.

Virtual Interviews

With the rise of remote work, virtual interviews have become increasingly common. They can be one-on-one, panel, or group formats conducted via video conferencing.

Strategies for Success:

1. Test your technology
Ensure your internet connection, camera, and microphone are working well before the interview.

2. Choose an appropriate background
Select a clean, professional-looking space for your video call. Virtual backgrounds can be used if necessary.

3. Dress professionally
Dress as you would for an in-person interview, from head to toe.

4. Make "eye contact" by looking at the camera
This helps create a connection with the interviewer(s).

5. Minimize distractions
Inform household members about your interview, silence notifications, and remove pets from the room.

6. Have a backup plan
Be prepared with a phone number to call in case of technical difficulties.

General Tips for All Interview Formats

Regardless of the interview format, certain strategies apply universally:

1. Prepare thoroughly

Research the company, practice common interview questions, and prepare your own questions.

2. Arrive early

Whether it's logging onto a virtual platform or arriving at a physical location, be ready at least 10 minutes before the scheduled time.

3. Bring necessary materials

Have copies of your resume, a notepad, and a pen. For virtual interviews, have these items within reach.

4. Follow up

Send a thank-you note or email within 24 hours of the interview, regardless of the format.

5. Stay positive

Maintain a positive attitude throughout the interview, even if you feel it's not going well.

6. Be authentic

While adapting to different formats is important, always remain true to yourself and your values.

7. Practice active listening

Regardless of the format, showing that you're fully engaged and listening carefully is crucial.

Conclusion

Each interview format presents its own set of challenges and opportunities.

CHAPTER 10: NAVIGATING DIFFERENT INTERVIEW FORMATS:...

By understanding the nuances of one-on-one, panel, and group interviews, you can adapt your approach to showcase your strengths effectively in any situation.

Remember, the key to success in any interview format is thorough preparation, adaptability, and authenticity. Practice navigating different interview scenarios, perhaps through mock interviews with friends or mentors. This will help you feel more comfortable and confident, regardless of the format you encounter.

As you prepare for your interviews, consider the company and role you're applying for. Some industries or positions may be more likely to use certain interview formats. If possible, ask your contact at the company about the expected interview format so you can prepare accordingly.

In the next chapter, we'll delve into the increasingly important world of virtual interviews, providing detailed strategies for making a strong impression in the digital space.

Chapter 11: Virtual Interviews: Excelling in the Digital Space

In recent years, virtual interviews have become increasingly prevalent, accelerated by global events and the rise of remote work. As companies embrace digital recruitment processes, mastering the art of the virtual interview has become essential for job seekers. This chapter will guide you through the nuances of excelling in virtual interviews, ensuring you make a strong impression in the digital space.

Understanding the Virtual Interview Landscape

Virtual interviews can take various forms:

1. Video interviews: Live conversations conducted through platforms like Zoom, Skype, or Microsoft Teams.
2. One-way video interviews: Pre-recorded responses to provided questions.
3. Phone interviews: Audio-only conversations, often used for initial screenings.

Each format requires slightly different preparation and techniques.

CHAPTER 11: VIRTUAL INTERVIEWS: EXCELLING IN THE DIGITAL...

Setting Up Your Virtual Interview Space

Creating the right environment is crucial for a successful virtual interview:

1. Choose a quiet, well-lit location
   Select a space with minimal background noise and distractions. Ensure the lighting is adequate and flattering, ideally with natural light facing you.

2. Set up a professional background
   Choose a neutral, uncluttered background. If using a virtual background, ensure it's professional and not distracting.

3. Position your camera correctly
   Place your camera at eye level. This typically means elevating your laptop on a stack of books or using a separate webcam.

4. Test your technology
   Check your internet connection, camera, microphone, and chosen video platform well in advance. Conduct a test call with a friend if possible.

5. Have a backup plan
   Be prepared with a phone number to call in case of technical difficulties.

Mastering Your Digital Presence

How you present yourself on camera can significantly impact the interviewer's perception:

1. Dress professionally
   Dress as you would for an in-person interview, from head to toe. Avoid busy patterns or bright colors that may not translate well on camera.

2. Make "eye contact" by looking at the camera

This creates the illusion of eye contact for the interviewer. Place a small sticker near your camera as a reminder to look there.

3. Use good posture
Sit up straight and lean slightly forward to appear engaged.

4. Minimize movements
Excessive movement can be distracting on video. Try to stay relatively still, using hand gestures sparingly and purposefully.

5. Smile and show enthusiasm
Your energy may not translate as well through video, so make an extra effort to appear enthusiastic and engaged.

Effective Communication in Virtual Interviews

Clear, effective communication is even more critical in a virtual setting:

1. Speak clearly and at a moderate pace
Be mindful of potential audio delays. Pause briefly after the interviewer speaks to ensure you don't interrupt.

2. Use the mute button wisely
Mute yourself when the interviewer is speaking for extended periods to eliminate background noise.

3. Prepare for silence
Don't be unnerved by silent pauses. They're often longer in virtual conversations due to slight delays.

4. Practice active listening
Nod and use facial expressions to show you're engaged, as the interviewer can't pick up on as many non-verbal cues.

CHAPTER 11: VIRTUAL INTERVIEWS: EXCELLING IN THE DIGITAL...

5. Have notes handy, but don't rely on them too heavily

It's okay to have a few notes out of frame, but maintain eye contact with the camera as much as possible.

Navigating One-Way Video Interviews

One-way video interviews present unique challenges:

1. Practice, practice, practice

Record yourself answering common interview questions to get comfortable with the format.

2. Pay attention to time limits

Many one-way interviews have strict time limits for each response. Practice timing your answers.

3. Show personality

Without the back-and-forth of a live conversation, it's crucial to inject energy and personality into your responses.

4. Use the preparation time wisely

Many platforms offer a short preparation time before each question. Use this to gather your thoughts and plan your response.

5. Remember your audience

Even though you're talking to a camera, imagine you're speaking directly to a person to maintain a conversational tone.

Handling Technical Difficulties

Technical issues can arise even with the best preparation:

1. Stay calm

Your reaction to technical difficulties can demonstrate your problem-solving skills and ability to handle stress.

2. Have a backup device ready
Be prepared to switch to a phone or tablet if your primary device fails.

3. Know how to troubleshoot common issues
Familiarize yourself with basic troubleshooting for audio and video problems.

4. Communicate promptly
If you're experiencing issues, let the interviewer know immediately. They will appreciate your proactive communication.

Virtual Interview Etiquette

Some etiquette rules are unique to virtual interviews:

1. Log in early
Join the virtual meeting room 5-10 minutes early to ensure everything is working properly.

2. Close unnecessary programs and browser tabs
This reduces the risk of slowdowns and eliminates potential notification sounds.

3. Turn off notifications
Silence your phone and turn off computer notifications to avoid distractions.

4. Have a glass of water nearby
Keep hydrated, but avoid eating during the interview.

5. Inform household members
Ensure roommates or family members know you're in an interview to prevent interruptions.

Following Up After a Virtual Interview

The follow-up process for virtual interviews is similar to in-person interviews:

1. Send a thank-you email within 24 hours
Reference specific points from the conversation to personalize your message.

2. Address any technical issues
If there were any significant technical problems, briefly apologize and offer to provide any information that may have been missed.

3. Reiterate your interest
Use the follow-up as an opportunity to reaffirm your enthusiasm for the position.

Preparing for the Future of Interviews

As technology evolves, so too will virtual interview practices:

1. Stay informed about new interview technologies
Be prepared for innovations like VR interviews or AI-driven assessments.

2. Continuously improve your digital communication skills
Practice video calls with friends or mentors to enhance your virtual presence.

3. Embrace the advantages of virtual interviews

Recognize the benefits, such as the ability to interview for positions anywhere in the world.

Conclusion

Virtual interviews, while presenting unique challenges, also offer opportunities to showcase your adaptability and digital communication skills. By creating a professional environment, mastering your on-camera presence, communicating effectively, and being prepared for technical challenges, you can excel in the digital interview space.

Remember, the core principles of interviewing still apply in a virtual setting. Thorough preparation, genuine enthusiasm, and clear articulation of your value proposition remain crucial. The virtual format simply adds an extra layer to consider in your presentation and interaction.

As the job market continues to evolve, your ability to navigate virtual interviews successfully will be an increasingly valuable skill. Embrace this format as an opportunity to demonstrate your adaptability and tech-savviness – qualities that are highly prized in today's rapidly changing work environment.

In the next chapter, we'll explore how to excel in behavioral interviews, where your past experiences and actions are used to predict your future performance.

Chapter 12: Behavioral Interviews: Proving You're the Perfect Fit

Behavioral interviews have become increasingly popular among employers as a way to assess candidates' suitability for a role based on their past experiences and actions. The premise is simple: past behavior is the best predictor of future performance. In this chapter, we'll explore how to excel in behavioral interviews, demonstrating that you're the perfect fit for the position through concrete examples from your professional history.

Understanding Behavioral Interviews

Behavioral interview questions typically start with phrases like:
    - "Tell me about a time when…"
    - "Describe a situation where…"
    - "Give me an example of…"

These questions are designed to elicit specific examples of how you've handled various work situations in the past. The interviewer is looking for evidence of skills and qualities that are important for the role.

The STAR Method: Your Secret Weapon

The STAR method is an effective framework for answering behavioral questions:

S - Situation: Set the context for your story.
   T - Task: Explain the challenge or responsibility you faced.
   A - Action: Describe the specific steps you took.
   R - Result: Share the outcomes and what you learned.

Using this method ensures your answers are structured, concise, and complete.

Preparing for Behavioral Interviews

1. Analyze the job description
   Identify the key skills and qualities the employer is seeking. Common areas include:
   - Leadership
   - Teamwork
   - Problem-solving
   - Adaptability
   - Communication
   - Conflict resolution

2. Reflect on your experiences
   For each key skill, think of 2-3 specific examples from your professional history that demonstrate your proficiency.

3. Prepare your STAR stories
   Develop concise narratives for each example using the STAR method. Practice telling these stories so they flow naturally.

4. Quantify results where possible
   Include specific metrics or data to illustrate the impact of your actions.

CHAPTER 12: BEHAVIORAL INTERVIEWS: PROVING YOU'RE THE...

5. Be ready to adapt

Prepare to modify your examples to fit different questions.

Common Behavioral Questions and How to Answer Them

1. Leadership: "Describe a time when you led a team through a difficult project."

STAR Example:

Situation: At my previous company, we were tasked with implementing a new CRM system across all departments.

Task: As project lead, I needed to ensure a smooth transition while minimizing disruption to daily operations.

Action: I formed a cross-functional team, created a detailed implementation plan, and conducted regular check-ins. I also developed a comprehensive training program for all employees.

Result: We completed the implementation two weeks ahead of schedule, and user adoption reached 95% within the first month, surpassing our goal of 80%.

2. Problem-solving: "Tell me about a time you faced an unexpected challenge at work and how you dealt with it."

STAR Example:

Situation: During a crucial product launch, our main supplier informed us of a significant delay in delivering key components.

Task: I needed to find an alternative solution to keep the launch on schedule.

Action: I quickly researched alternative suppliers, negotiated expedited shipping, and reorganized our assembly process to accommodate the change.

Result: We managed to launch on time, and the experience led us to diversify our supplier base, improving our supply chain resilience.

3. Teamwork: "Give an example of how you worked effectively as part of a team."

STAR Example:
Situation: Our marketing team was struggling to meet deadlines due to poor communication and unclear role definitions.
Task: As a team member, I saw an opportunity to improve our collaboration and efficiency.
Action: I proposed and implemented a project management tool, created clear workflow processes, and initiated weekly stand-up meetings.
Result: Our team's productivity increased by 30%, and we consistently met deadlines for the next six months.

4. Adaptability: "Describe a situation where you had to adapt to a significant change at work."

STAR Example:
Situation: My company underwent a merger, resulting in a complete restructuring of my department.
Task: I needed to adjust to new leadership, different processes, and a shifted focus in my role.
Action: I proactively scheduled meetings with new team members, volunteered for cross-departmental projects, and took online courses to fill skill gaps.
Result: Within three months, I became a go-to person for bridging communication between old and new teams, and I was promoted to a team lead position in the new structure.

5. Conflict Resolution: "Tell me about a time you had to resolve a conflict with a coworker."

STAR Example:
Situation: I disagreed with a colleague over the approach to a major client

presentation.

Task: We needed to find a resolution quickly to meet the presentation deadline.

Action: I suggested we meet privately to discuss our concerns. I practiced active listening to understand their perspective and proposed a compromise that incorporated both our ideas.

Result: We delivered a successful presentation that the client praised for its comprehensive approach. This experience improved our working relationship and led to more collaborative efforts in the future.

Tips for Excelling in Behavioral Interviews

1. Be specific

Provide detailed examples rather than general statements. The interviewer wants to hear about real situations you've faced.

2. Be honest

Don't invent stories or exaggerate your role. Authenticity is key, and experienced interviewers can often detect embellishments.

3. Choose relevant examples

Select stories that closely relate to the skills required for the position you're seeking.

4. Show growth

When possible, include what you learned from the experience and how you've applied those lessons since.

5. Be prepared for follow-up questions

The interviewer may ask for additional details or clarification. Be ready to expand on your examples.

6. Practice active listening

Ensure you fully understand the question before answering. It's okay to ask for clarification if needed.

7. Keep it professional
While your examples should be personal, avoid overly personal information or negative comments about former employers or colleagues.

8. Use "I" statements
Even when discussing team efforts, focus on your specific contributions and actions.

9. Be concise
Aim to keep your responses to 2-3 minutes. If the interviewer wants more details, they'll ask.

10. Show enthusiasm
Your tone and body language should convey genuine interest in the experiences you're sharing.

Handling Difficult Behavioral Questions

1. If you can't think of an example
It's okay to take a moment to think. You can say, "That's an interesting question. Let me think of the best example." If you truly can't recall a relevant situation, explain how you would handle such a scenario hypothetically.

2. If asked about a failure
Be honest about the situation, but focus on what you learned and how you've grown from the experience.

3. If the question is unclear
Don't hesitate to ask for clarification. It's better to fully understand the question than to provide an irrelevant answer.

Conclusion

Behavioral interviews offer a fantastic opportunity to showcase your skills and experiences in a concrete, impactful way. By preparing thoughtful STAR examples that align with the job requirements, you can effectively demonstrate that you're the perfect fit for the role.

Remember, the key to success in behavioral interviews is preparation, authenticity, and the ability to connect your past experiences to the potential challenges of the new position. With practice and the right mindset, you can turn these interviews into powerful platforms for highlighting your unique value proposition.

In the next chapter, we'll explore technical interviews, providing strategies for demonstrating your expertise in specialized fields.

Chapter 13: Technical Interviews: Demonstrating Your Expertise

Technical interviews are a crucial part of the hiring process for many specialized roles, particularly in fields like software engineering, data science, IT, and other technology-related positions. These interviews are designed to assess your technical skills, problem-solving abilities, and depth of knowledge in your area of expertise. In this chapter, we'll explore strategies for excelling in technical interviews and demonstrating your expertise effectively.

Understanding Technical Interviews

Technical interviews can take various forms:

1. Coding challenges: Writing code to solve specific problems.
2. System design questions: Designing large-scale systems or architectures.
3. Algorithm and data structure questions: Solving complex problems efficiently.
4. Domain-specific questions: Demonstrating knowledge in your particular field.
5. Whiteboarding sessions: Explaining your thought process while solving problems.

6. Take-home assignments: Completing a project within a given timeframe.

Preparing for Technical Interviews

1. Review fundamentals
Revisit core concepts in your field, such as data structures, algorithms, design patterns, or domain-specific principles.

2. Practice coding
Use platforms like LeetCode, HackerRank, or CodeSignal to practice coding challenges.

3. Study system design
For more senior roles, understand how to design scalable, efficient systems.

4. Stay current
Keep up with the latest trends, technologies, and best practices in your field.

5. Review your past projects
Be prepared to discuss your previous work in detail.

6. Prepare questions
Have thoughtful questions ready about the company's technical challenges and processes.

Strategies for Excelling in Technical Interviews

1. Understand the problem before coding
Take time to clarify the requirements and constraints. Ask questions if needed.

Example dialogue:
Interviewer: "Write a function to find the nth Fibonacci number."
You: "Certainly. Before I begin, could you clarify if you're looking for a recursive or iterative solution? Also, should I consider optimizations for large values of n?"

2. Think aloud
Verbalize your thought process. This gives the interviewer insight into how you approach problems.

Example:
"I'm thinking of using a dynamic programming approach here to optimize the time complexity. Let me start by defining the base cases…"

3. Start with a brute force solution
Begin with a simple solution, then optimize. This shows you can produce working code quickly and then improve it.

Example:
"I'll start with a simple recursive solution to demonstrate the logic, then we can discuss how to optimize it using memoization or an iterative approach."

4. Analyze time and space complexity
Discuss the efficiency of your solution in terms of big O notation.

Example:
"This solution has a time complexity of $O(n)$ and a space complexity of $O(1)$. We've achieved linear time complexity by using an iterative approach instead of recursion."

5. Test your code
After writing your solution, walk through it with test cases, including edge cases.

Example:
"Let's test this with a few cases. For n=0, we expect 0. For n=1, we expect 1. Let's also try a larger number, say n=10, which should give us 55."

6. Optimize and improve
If time allows, discuss potential optimizations or alternative approaches.

Example:
"We could further optimize this by using matrix exponentiation, which would reduce the time complexity to $O(\log n)$. Would you like me to implement that?"

7. Ask for feedback
After completing a problem, ask if there are any areas for improvement.

Handling Different Types of Technical Questions

1. Coding Challenges

Approach:
- Clarify requirements
- Discuss your approach before coding
- Write clean, well-commented code
- Test your solution

Example:
Interviewer: "Implement a function to reverse a linked list."

You: "Certainly. I'll implement this iteratively to achieve $O(n)$ time complexity and $O(1)$ space complexity. Here's the approach:

```python
def reverse_linked_list(head):
```

```
prev = None
current = head
while current:
    next_node = current.next
    current.next = prev
    prev = current
    current = next_node
return prev

# Test cases
# ... [implement test cases]
"""
```

This solution reverses the links in place, using three pointers to keep track of the previous, current, and next nodes."

2. System Design Questions

Approach:
   - Clarify requirements and scale
   - Start with a high-level design
   - Dive into specific components
   - Discuss trade-offs

Example:
   Interviewer: "Design a URL shortening service like bit.ly."

You: "Let's approach this step by step:

1. Requirements:
   - Shorten long URLs
   - Redirect users to original URL
   - Handle high traffic

CHAPTER 13: TECHNICAL INTERVIEWS: DEMONSTRATING YOUR...

   - Minimize latency

2. High-level design:
   - Web server to handle requests
   - Database to store URL mappings
   - Caching layer for frequently accessed URLs

3. Detailed design:
   - Hash function to generate short URLs
   - Database schema: (short_url, original_url, creation_date, user_id)
   - Load balancer for distributed traffic

4. Scalability considerations:
   - Partitioning strategy for database
   - Replication for fault tolerance
   - CDN for global access

Would you like me to elaborate on any specific component?"

3. Algorithm and Data Structure Questions

Approach:
   - Identify the appropriate data structure
   - Explain your choice
   - Implement the solution
   - Analyze complexity

Example:
   Interviewer: "Implement a Least Recently Used (LRU) cache."

You: "For an LRU cache, we need fast access and efficient updates. I'll use a hash map for O(1) access and a doubly linked list for O(1) updates. Here's the basic structure:

```python
class LRUCache:
    def __init__(self, capacity):
        self.capacity = capacity
        self.cache = {}
        self.list = DoublyLinkedList()

def get(self, key):
    if key in self.cache:
        node = self.cache[key]
        self.list.move_to_front(node)
        return node.value
    return -1

def put(self, key, value):
    if key in self.cache:
        node = self.cache[key]
        node.value = value
        self.list.move_to_front(node)
    else:
        if len(self.cache) >= self.capacity:
            lru_key = self.list.remove_tail()
            del self.cache[lru_key]
        new_node = ListNode(key, value)
        self.list.add_to_front(new_node)
        self.cache[key] = new_node

# Additional implementation details...
```

This design gives us O(1) time complexity for both get and put operations."

4. Domain-Specific Questions

Approach:
  - Demonstrate depth of knowledge
  - Provide real-world examples
  - Discuss trade-offs and best practices

Example (for a data science role):
Interviewer: "Explain the difference between L1 and L2 regularization in machine learning."

You: "L1 and L2 regularization are techniques used to prevent overfitting in machine learning models.

L1 regularization (Lasso):
  - Adds the absolute value of coefficients to the loss function
  - Tends to produce sparse models by driving some coefficients to zero
  - Useful for feature selection

L2 regularization (Ridge):
  - Adds the squared value of coefficients to the loss function
  - Tends to shrink coefficients uniformly
  - Better for dealing with multicollinearity

In practice, I've used L1 regularization in a project where we needed to identify the most impactful features in a high-dimensional dataset for predicting customer churn. L2 regularization was more appropriate in a different project where we had correlated features in a linear regression model for house price prediction."

Conclusion

Technical interviews can be challenging, but with thorough preparation and effective communication of your thought process, you can demonstrate your expertise convincingly. Remember to:

- Practice regularly
  - Stay calm and composed
  - Communicate clearly
  - Be open to feedback
  - Show enthusiasm for problem-solving

By following these strategies, you'll be well-equipped to showcase your technical skills and stand out as a top candidate in your field.

Chapter 14: Salary Negotiations: Knowing Your Worth and Getting It

Salary negotiation is a crucial part of the job search process, yet it's often the most uncomfortable for many candidates. However, mastering the art of salary negotiation can significantly impact your earning potential and career satisfaction. This chapter will guide you through the process of understanding your worth and effectively negotiating your compensation package.

Understanding the Importance of Salary Negotiation

1. Long-term impact: Your starting salary sets the baseline for future raises and bonuses.
2. Professional value: It reflects how your skills and experience are valued in the market.
3. Job satisfaction: Fair compensation contributes to overall job satisfaction and motivation.

Preparing for Salary Negotiations

1. Research Industry Standards
    - Use websites like Glassdoor, PayScale, and Salary.com to research salary

ranges for your position and location.
   - Consult professional associations in your field for salary surveys.
   - Network with colleagues to gain insights into current market rates.

2. Assess Your Value
   - List your unique skills, experiences, and achievements.
   - Consider factors like education, certifications, and specialized training.
   - Quantify your contributions in previous roles (e.g., increased sales by 20%, reduced costs by $100,000).

3. Understand the Complete Compensation Package
   - Base salary
   - Bonuses and profit-sharing
   - Stock options or equity
   - Health and retirement benefits
   - Paid time off
   - Professional development opportunities
   - Flexible working arrangements

4. Determine Your Salary Range
   - Set a target salary based on your research and assessment.
   - Establish your "walk away" number – the minimum you're willing to accept.

5. Practice Your Pitch
   - Prepare a concise statement of your value proposition.
   - Practice with a friend or mentor to gain confidence.

Timing Your Salary Discussion

1. Avoid Discussing Salary Too Early
   - Ideally, let the employer bring up compensation first.
   - If asked about salary expectations early, deflect with a statement like: "I'm

CHAPTER 14: SALARY NEGOTIATIONS: KNOWING YOUR WORTH AND...

more interested in finding the right fit. Can we discuss salary after we've determined I'm the right candidate for the role?"

2. Wait Until You Have Leverage
   - Ideally, negotiate after you've received a job offer.
   - At this point, the employer has invested time in you and wants to close the deal.

Negotiation Strategies

1. Let the Employer Make the First Offer
   - This gives you valuable information and prevents you from undervaluing yourself.

2. Don't Accept the First Offer
   - Even if the offer is good, it's usually acceptable to negotiate.
   - Example response: "Thank you for the offer. I'm excited about the opportunity to join your team. Based on my research and experience, I was expecting a salary in the range of [your target]. Can we discuss this further?"

3. Focus on Your Value
   - Highlight your unique skills and experiences that justify your salary request.
   - Example: "Given my track record of increasing sales by 30% in my previous role and my expertise in [specific skill], I believe a salary of [your target] aligns with the value I'll bring to the company."

4. Use Silence Effectively
   - After stating your case, resist the urge to fill silence. Let the employer respond.

5. Be Prepared to Compromise

- If the employer can't meet your salary request, consider negotiating other benefits.
- Example: "I understand that [your target salary] might not be possible at this time. Could we discuss additional vacation days or a performance review in six months?"

6. Get the Offer in Writing
- Once you've reached an agreement, ask for the final offer in writing to avoid any misunderstandings.

Handling Common Scenarios

1. When Asked About Salary History
- Many locations have banned this question, but if legal and asked, redirect the conversation.
- Example response: "I'd prefer to focus on the value I can bring to this role and discuss a salary that's fair for the position's responsibilities."

2. When Faced with a Salary Range
- Aim for the higher end of the range, justifying it with your qualifications.
- Example: "Given my 10 years of experience and proven track record, I believe a salary at the upper end of that range at [specific amount] would be appropriate."

3. When Negotiating a Raise in Your Current Job
- Timing is crucial. Consider your company's financial health and your recent achievements.
- Prepare a "brag sheet" documenting your accomplishments and their impact on the company.
- Example opener: "I've been consistently exceeding my targets and have taken on additional responsibilities. I'd like to discuss adjusting my compensation to reflect my increased contributions to the team."

4. When the Employer Can't Budge on Salary
   - Explore other forms of compensation.
   - Example: "I understand that the budget for the base salary is fixed. Could we discuss a signing bonus or a performance-based bonus structure?"

5. When You Receive Multiple Offers
   - Use this as leverage, but be tactful.
   - Example: "I've received another offer with a higher salary, but I'm really excited about the opportunity with your company. Is there any flexibility in the compensation package?"

Negotiation Don'ts

1. Don't Lie About Other Offers or Your Current Salary
   - Dishonesty can damage your professional reputation.

2. Don't Make Ultimatums Unless You're Prepared to Walk Away
   - Threats can sour the negotiation process.

3. Don't Focus Solely on Salary
   - Consider the entire compensation package and career growth opportunities.

4. Don't Apologize for Negotiating
   - It's a normal and expected part of the hiring process.

5. Don't Forget to Get the Final Offer in Writing
   - Verbal agreements can be misremembered or misinterpreted.

Closing the Deal

1. Express Gratitude
   - Thank the employer for their time and consideration, regardless of the

outcome.

2. Confirm Next Steps
   - Ensure you understand the timeline for making a decision and starting the role.

3. Get Everything in Writing
   - Review the written offer carefully before accepting.

4. Maintain Professionalism
   - Even if you decide to decline, keep the door open for future opportunities.

Example Closing Statement: "Thank you for working with me on this. I'm excited about the opportunity and the agreed-upon compensation package. I look forward to receiving the official offer letter and joining the team."

Conclusion

Salary negotiation is a skill that can significantly impact your career trajectory and job satisfaction. By thoroughly preparing, understanding your worth, and approaching the negotiation with confidence and professionalism, you can secure a compensation package that reflects your value.

Remember, negotiation is not about winning or losing, but about finding a mutually beneficial agreement. Employers expect candidates to negotiate, and doing so respectfully and confidently can actually increase their respect for you.

As you move forward in your career, continue to track your achievements and stay informed about market rates for your skills. This ongoing awareness will serve you well in future negotiations, whether for new positions or within your current role.

In the next chapter, we'll explore effective strategies for following up after the interview, ensuring you maintain a positive impression and increase your chances of landing the job.

Chapter 15: Following Up: The Post-Interview Strategy That Sets You Apart

The interview process doesn't end when you walk out of the room or log off the video call. A well-executed follow-up strategy can reinforce your candidacy, demonstrate your enthusiasm for the position, and potentially tip the scales in your favor. This chapter will guide you through effective post-interview follow-up techniques that can set you apart from other candidates.

The Importance of Following Up

1. Demonstrates professionalism and courtesy
2. Keeps you fresh in the interviewer's mind
3. Provides an opportunity to reiterate your interest and qualifications
4. Allows you to address any points you may have missed during the interview
5. Shows initiative and strong communication skills

Timing Your Follow-Up

1. Send a thank-you email within 24 hours

CHAPTER 15: FOLLOWING UP: THE POST-INTERVIEW STRATEGY THAT...

This immediate follow-up shows promptness and enthusiasm.

2. If you haven't heard back within the specified timeframe, wait an additional 3-5 business days before following up again
This demonstrates patience while still showing interest.

3. If you need to make a decision on another offer, it's appropriate to reach out and inquire about your status
Be polite and provide a specific deadline if you have one.

The Thank-You Email

The thank-you email is your first and most crucial follow-up communication. Here's how to craft an effective one:

1. Personalize the email
Address the interviewer by name and reference specific points from your conversation.

2. Express gratitude
Thank them for their time and the opportunity to learn more about the role and company.

3. Reiterate your interest and qualifications
Briefly remind them why you're a great fit for the position.

4. Address any unresolved issues
If there was a question you struggled with or a point you didn't get to make, you can briefly address it here.

5. Provide any requested information
If you promised to send additional information, include it or let them know when they can expect it.

6. Close with a call to action
   Express your eagerness to hear about the next steps in the process.

Example Thank-You Email:

"""

Subject: Thank you for the [Position] interview

Dear [Interviewer's Name],

Thank you for taking the time to meet with me yesterday regarding the [Position] role at [Company Name]. I enjoyed our conversation and am even more excited about the opportunity to join your team.

I was particularly intrigued by your plans for [specific project or initiative discussed]. My experience with [relevant skill or project] aligns well with this initiative, and I'm confident I can contribute significantly to its success.

As we discussed, I've attached the portfolio of my recent projects that demonstrate my expertise in [relevant area]. Please let me know if you need any additional information.

I'm looking forward to hearing about the next steps in the process. Thank you again for your time and consideration.

Best regards,
   [Your Name]
   """

Following Up After No Response

If you haven't heard back within the specified timeframe, it's appropriate to send a polite follow-up email:

CHAPTER 15: FOLLOWING UP: THE POST-INTERVIEW STRATEGY THAT...

1. Reference your previous communication
2. Reiterate your interest in the position
3. Ask about the status of your application
4. Offer to provide any additional information

Example Follow-Up Email:

"""

Subject: Following up on [Position] application

Dear [Interviewer's Name],

I hope this email finds you well. I wanted to follow up on my application for the [Position] role, which we discussed in our interview on [date]. I remain very interested in this opportunity and am eager to learn about the next steps in the process.

Has there been any update on the status of my application? If you need any additional information from me, please don't hesitate to ask.

Thank you again for your time and consideration.

Best regards,
  [Your Name]
"""

Staying in Touch

If the hiring process is prolonged, or even if you don't get the job, staying in touch can be beneficial:

1. Connect on LinkedIn

Send a personalized connection request mentioning your interview.

2. Share relevant articles or information

If you come across something relevant to your discussion, share it with a brief note.

3. Provide updates on your achievements

If you accomplish something significant related to your discussion, let them know.

Example LinkedIn Message:

"

Dear [Interviewer's Name],

It was a pleasure meeting you during my interview for the [Position] role at [Company Name]. I'd like to stay connected and keep up with the exciting work your team is doing.

I recently read an article about [relevant topic] that reminded me of our discussion about [specific point]. I thought you might find it interesting: [link]

Thank you again for your time and insights.

Best regards,
  [Your Name]
  "

Following Up After Receiving an Offer

If you receive a job offer, your follow-up should:

CHAPTER 15: FOLLOWING UP: THE POST-INTERVIEW STRATEGY THAT...

1. Express gratitude for the offer
2. Confirm the details (salary, start date, etc.)
3. Ask about the deadline for your decision
4. Request any additional information you need to make your decision

Example Offer Follow-Up:

"""

Dear [Hiring Manager's Name],

Thank you for offering me the position of [Job Title] at [Company Name]. I'm excited about the opportunity and appreciate your confidence in me.

I would like to confirm the details of the offer:
 - Start date: [Date]
 - Salary: [Amount]
 - Benefits: [List key benefits]

Could you please let me know by when you need my decision? Also, I had a few questions about [specific aspect of the job or benefits]. Would it be possible to schedule a brief call to discuss these?

Thank you again for this opportunity. I look forward to your response.

Best regards,
  [Your Name]
"""

Following Up After Rejection

Even if you don't get the job, a gracious follow-up can leave a positive impression and potentially lead to future opportunities:

1. Thank them for their time and the opportunity
2. Express your disappointment professionally
3. Ask for feedback if appropriate
4. Leave the door open for future opportunities

Example Rejection Follow-Up:

"

Dear [Interviewer's Name],

Thank you for informing me of your decision regarding the [Position] role. While I'm disappointed not to be moving forward, I appreciated the opportunity to learn more about [Company Name] and meet with you and your team.

I would be grateful for any feedback you could provide on my interview or qualifications. This insight would be valuable for my professional development.

I remain impressed with [Company Name] and would welcome the opportunity to be considered for future roles that might be a good fit. Please feel free to keep my resume on file.

Thank you again for your time and consideration.

Best regards,
[Your Name]
"

Conclusion

A thoughtful, well-executed follow-up strategy can significantly enhance

CHAPTER 15: FOLLOWING UP: THE POST-INTERVIEW STRATEGY THAT...

your chances of landing the job and leave a lasting positive impression, even if you're not selected for this particular role. Remember, the key elements of effective follow-up are:

1. Timeliness
2. Personalization
3. Professionalism
4. Genuine interest and enthusiasm
5. Conciseness and clarity

By mastering the art of following up, you demonstrate your communication skills, reinforce your interest in the position, and set yourself apart as a candidate who goes the extra mile. Even if you don't secure this particular job, your professional follow-up can leave a positive impression that may lead to future opportunities.

In the next chapter, we'll explore how to handle rejection constructively, turning a 'no' into a valuable learning experience and potential future 'yes'.

Chapter 16: Handling Rejection: Turning a 'No' into a Future 'Yes'

Rejection is an inevitable part of the job search process. Even the most qualified candidates face rejection at some point in their careers. However, the way you handle rejection can significantly impact your future opportunities and professional growth. This chapter will guide you through the process of turning a 'no' into a potential future 'yes', helping you maintain a positive outlook and leverage rejection as a stepping stone to success.

Understanding Rejection

1. It's not personal
   Rejection often has more to do with factors beyond your control, such as internal candidates, budget constraints, or changing company needs.

2. It's a common experience
   Even highly successful professionals have faced rejection in their careers.

3. It's an opportunity for growth
   Each rejection can provide valuable insights and opportunities for improvement.

The Immediate Aftermath: Processing Rejection

CHAPTER 16: HANDLING REJECTION: TURNING A 'NO' INTO A FUTURE...

1. Allow yourself to feel disappointed
   It's natural and healthy to acknowledge your feelings.

2. Avoid negative self-talk
   Don't let rejection undermine your self-worth or confidence.

3. Maintain perspective
   Remember that this is just one opportunity out of many in your career.

4. Practice self-care
   Engage in activities that boost your mood and confidence.

Turning Rejection into a Learning Experience

1. Request feedback
   Reach out to the hiring manager or recruiter for constructive feedback.

Example email:

"""

Dear [Hiring Manager's Name],

Thank you for informing me of your decision regarding the [Position] role. While I'm disappointed not to be moving forward, I valued the opportunity to learn more about [Company Name] and meet with you and your team.

I'm committed to continuous improvement in my professional development. With that in mind, I would greatly appreciate any feedback you could provide on my interview performance or qualifications. Your insights would be invaluable in helping me grow and prepare for future opportunities.

Thank you again for your time and consideration.

Best regards,
   [Your Name]
   "

2. Analyze your performance
   Reflect on the interview process and identify areas for improvement.

3. Identify skill gaps
   Determine if there are skills or qualifications you need to develop.

4. Seek mentorship
   Discuss your experience with a mentor or trusted colleague for additional insights.

Maintaining Professional Relationships

1. Respond graciously to rejection
   Thank the company for their time and consideration.

2. Express continued interest
   Let them know you'd be open to future opportunities.

3. Stay connected
   Follow the company and key individuals on professional networking platforms.

4. Provide occasional updates
   Share relevant professional achievements or articles of interest.

Example LinkedIn message:

"

   Dear [Interviewer's Name],

CHAPTER 16: HANDLING REJECTION: TURNING A 'NO' INTO A FUTURE...

I hope this message finds you well. I wanted to touch base and share that I recently completed a certification in [relevant area] that we discussed during my interview for the [Position] role. While I understand that position has been filled, I remain very interested in opportunities with [Company Name] and would welcome the chance to discuss any suitable roles that may arise in the future.

I continue to follow [Company Name]'s exciting developments and was particularly impressed by the recent announcement of [specific company news or achievement].

Thank you again for your time and consideration. I look forward to staying in touch.

Best regards,
   [Your Name]
   "

Leveraging Rejection for Future Success

1. Use the experience to refine your job search
   Adjust your approach based on what you've learned.

2. Enhance your qualifications
   Address any skill gaps identified through feedback or self-reflection.

3. Expand your network
   Maintain connections with interviewers and other professionals you met during the process.

4. Improve your interview skills
   Use insights gained to better prepare for future interviews.

5. Refine your career goals
Use the experience to clarify what you're looking for in your next role.

Staying Motivated During the Job Search

1. Set small, achievable goals
Break your job search into manageable tasks to maintain a sense of progress.

2. Celebrate small wins
Acknowledge each step forward, such as securing an interview or receiving positive feedback.

3. Maintain a routine
Treat your job search like a job itself, with regular hours and structured activities.

4. Diversify your efforts
Don't put all your eggs in one basket; pursue multiple opportunities simultaneously.

5. Stay active in your field
Attend industry events, take courses, or engage in volunteer work to stay connected and motivated.

Turning Rejection into Opportunity: Success Stories

Share these examples with yourself or others facing rejection:

1. The Persistent Candidate
After being rejected for her dream job, Sarah stayed in touch with the company, sharing relevant industry insights and her professional achievements. Six months later, when a similar position opened up, the hiring manager

CHAPTER 16: HANDLING REJECTION: TURNING A 'NO' INTO A FUTURE...

reached out to her directly, leading to a successful hire.

2. The Skill Developer

Tom was rejected due to a lack of specific technical skills. He used this feedback to enroll in relevant courses and obtain certifications. When he applied to the same company a year later, he was hired for an even better position.

3. The Network Builder

Despite not getting the job, Maria maintained a positive relationship with the interviewer. This connection later introduced her to another opportunity in a different company, which turned out to be an even better fit for her career goals.

4. The Feedback Implementer

After receiving constructive feedback on his interview performance, Alex worked with a career coach to improve his communication skills. His next interview was a success, landing him a position he was initially unsure he was qualified for.

Conclusion

Rejection, while challenging, is not the end of your career journey—it's often just the beginning of a new chapter. By approaching rejection with a growth mindset, maintaining professionalism, and leveraging the experience for self-improvement, you can turn a 'no' into a valuable stepping stone towards future success.

Remember:

1. Every 'no' brings you closer to a 'yes'
2. Feedback is a gift—use it to grow and improve
3. Maintain relationships and stay connected—you never know where

they might lead
4. Use rejection as motivation to refine your skills and career goals
5. Stay positive and persistent—your ideal opportunity may be just around the corner

By mastering the art of handling rejection constructively, you not only improve your chances of future success but also demonstrate resilience and professionalism—qualities highly valued by employers. In the face of rejection, choose growth, learning, and perseverance. Your future self will thank you for it.

Chapter 17: Interview Preparation Checklist: Your Step-by-Step Guide

A successful interview is the result of thorough preparation. This comprehensive checklist will guide you through each step of the interview preparation process, ensuring you're ready to make a strong impression and showcase your qualifications effectively.

1. Research the Company
    - ☐ Study the company's website, focusing on:
    - ☐ Mission statement and values
    - ☐ Products or services
    - ☐ Recent news and press releases
    - ☐ Leadership team

- ☐ Review the company's social media presence
    - ☐ Read recent annual reports (if publicly available)
    - ☐ Research the company's competitors and industry trends
    - ☐ Understand the company culture and work environment

2. Analyze the Job Description
    - ☐ Highlight key responsibilities and requirements
    - ☐ Identify specific skills and experiences the employer is seeking
    - ☐ Note any unique or standout aspects of the role
    - ☐ Prepare examples that demonstrate your fit for these key areas

3. Prepare Your Responses
    - ☐ Practice answers to common interview questions:
    - ☐ "Tell me about yourself"
    - ☐ "Why are you interested in this position?"
    - ☐ "What are your strengths and weaknesses?"
    - ☐ "Where do you see yourself in five years?"

☐ Develop STAR (Situation, Task, Action, Result) stories for behavioral questions
    - ☐ Prepare questions to ask the interviewer about the role and company

4. Review Your Resume and Application Materials
    - ☐ Refresh your memory on the details of your work history
    - ☐ Be prepared to explain any gaps in employment
    - ☐ Identify key achievements to highlight during the interview
    - ☐ Bring extra copies of your resume to the interview

5. Prepare for Different Interview Formats
    - ☐ One-on-one interviews
    - ☐ Panel interviews
    - ☐ Group interviews
    - ☐ Video interviews:
    - ☐ Test your technology
    - ☐ Set up a professional background
    - ☐ Ensure good lighting

6. Plan Your Attire
    - ☐ Choose appropriate professional attire for the company culture
    - ☐ Ensure your outfit is clean, pressed, and fits well
    - ☐ Polish your shoes
    - ☐ Minimize distracting jewelry or accessories
    - ☐ Prepare your outfit the night before

CHAPTER 17: INTERVIEW PREPARATION CHECKLIST: YOUR...

7. Gather Necessary Materials
   - ☐ Multiple copies of your resume
   - ☐ Notepad and pen
   - ☐ Portfolio of your work (if applicable)
   - ☐ List of references
   - ☐ Directions to the interview location or video conferencing link

8. Practice Good Non-Verbal Communication
   - ☐ Work on maintaining good eye contact
   - ☐ Practice a firm handshake
   - ☐ Be aware of your posture and body language
   - ☐ Rehearse your facial expressions, aiming for a pleasant and engaged look

9. Prepare for the Logistics
   - ☐ Confirm the date, time, and location of the interview
   - ☐ Plan your route and transportation
   - ☐ Aim to arrive 10-15 minutes early
   - ☐ For video interviews, log in 5-10 minutes early to check your setup

10. Research Your Interviewers
    - ☐ If possible, learn the names and roles of your interviewers
    - ☐ Review their LinkedIn profiles or professional bios
    - ☐ Prepare to address interviewers by name during the interview

11. Develop Your Personal Pitch
    - ☐ Craft a concise "elevator pitch" about your professional background and goals
    - ☐ Tailor this pitch to the specific role and company
    - ☐ Practice delivering your pitch naturally and confidently

12. Prepare for Salary Discussions
    - ☐ Research salary ranges for the position in your area
    - ☐ Determine your salary expectations and "walk away" number

☐ Prepare to discuss benefits and other forms of compensation

13. Review Industry and Role-Specific Knowledge
    ☐ Brush up on current trends and challenges in your industry
    ☐ Review technical skills or knowledge specific to the role
    ☐ Prepare examples of how you've applied this knowledge in past roles

14. Practice Active Listening
    ☐ Remind yourself to focus on fully understanding each question before answering
    ☐ Prepare to ask clarifying questions if needed
    ☐ Practice paraphrasing to ensure understanding

15. Develop a Strategy for Handling Difficult Questions
    ☐ Prepare for questions about employment gaps or job changes
    ☐ Practice discussing weaknesses or areas for improvement positively
    ☐ Develop strategies for addressing conflict-related questions

16. Plan Your Post-Interview Follow-Up
    ☐ Prepare a thank-you email template
    ☐ Gather contact information for follow-up communications
    ☐ Plan to send a thank-you note within 24 hours of the interview

17. Mental and Physical Preparation
    ☐ Get a good night's sleep before the interview
    ☐ Plan a healthy meal before the interview
    ☐ Practice relaxation or mindfulness techniques to manage anxiety
    ☐ Prepare a positive, confident mindset

18. Prepare for Remote Interviews (if applicable)
    ☐ Ensure your internet connection is stable
    ☐ Choose a quiet, well-lit location for the interview
    ☐ Test your camera and microphone

☐ Close unnecessary programs on your computer to avoid distractions

19. Review Company Products or Services
    ☐ If applicable, try the company's product or service
    ☐ Prepare thoughtful feedback or questions about the product/service

20. Prepare for Potential Assessments
    ☐ Research if the company typically includes skills assessments or tests
    ☐ Practice relevant skills or problem-solving techniques

21. Develop a Personal Branding Strategy
    ☐ Identify key messages about your professional brand to convey
    ☐ Prepare concise examples that illustrate your unique value proposition

22. Plan for the Unexpected
    ☐ Prepare strategies for handling unexpected questions or situations
    ☐ Have a backup plan for technology issues in virtual interviews
    ☐ Bring any medications you might need

23. Review Your Online Presence
    ☐ Ensure your LinkedIn profile is up-to-date and professional
    ☐ Review your social media accounts for any potentially problematic content
    ☐ Google yourself to see what information is publicly available

24. Practice Time Management
    ☐ Prepare concise responses to common questions
    ☐ Practice pacing yourself during mock interviews

25. Prepare to Close the Interview Strong
    ☐ Develop a closing statement that reiterates your interest and qualifications
    ☐ Prepare to ask about next steps in the hiring process

Final Check:
- ☐ Review this checklist the day before your interview
- ☐ Get a good night's sleep
- ☐ On the day of the interview, give yourself plenty of time to arrive or set up
- ☐ Take a deep breath and remind yourself of your preparation and qualifications

By following this comprehensive checklist, you'll be well-prepared for your interview. Remember, thorough preparation not only helps you perform better but also boosts your confidence, allowing your true qualifications and personality to shine through. Good luck with your interview!

Chapter 18: Industry-Specific Interview Tips: Tailoring Your Approach

While general interview preparation is crucial, tailoring your approach to the specific industry you're interviewing for can give you a significant edge. Each industry has its unique culture, challenges, and expectations. This chapter will provide industry-specific tips to help you customize your interview strategy for various sectors.

1. Technology and IT

- Demonstrate your technical skills: Be prepared for technical questions or coding challenges.
- Stay current: Discuss the latest trends, technologies, and programming languages relevant to the role.
- Show adaptability: Emphasize your ability to learn new technologies quickly.
- Highlight problem-solving skills: Provide examples of complex technical issues you've resolved.
- Discuss collaboration: Technology roles often involve teamwork, so emphasize your ability to work in cross-functional teams.

Example question: "Describe a time when you had to learn a new technology quickly to complete a project."

2. Finance and Banking

- Demonstrate market knowledge: Be prepared to discuss current financial trends and market conditions.
- Showcase analytical skills: Provide examples of financial analysis you've conducted.
- Emphasize attention to detail: Discuss your experience with compliance and regulatory requirements.
- Highlight risk management: Provide examples of how you've identified and mitigated financial risks.
- Discuss ethical decision-making: Be prepared to talk about how you handle ethical dilemmas.

Example question: "How do you stay informed about changes in financial regulations, and how have you applied this knowledge in your work?"

3. Healthcare

- Demonstrate patient-centric approach: Discuss how you prioritize patient care and safety.
- Showcase knowledge of healthcare regulations: Be familiar with HIPAA and other relevant regulations.
- Emphasize teamwork: Highlight your ability to work in multidisciplinary healthcare teams.
- Discuss continuous learning: Healthcare is always evolving, so emphasize your commitment to ongoing education.
- Highlight empathy and communication skills: These are crucial in healthcare settings.

Example question: "Describe a situation where you had to balance patient care with administrative responsibilities."

4. Education

- Showcase your teaching philosophy: Be prepared to discuss your approach to education and student engagement.
- Demonstrate adaptability: Discuss how you adjust your teaching methods for different learning styles.
- Highlight classroom management skills: Provide examples of how you create a positive learning environment.
- Discuss assessment strategies: Be prepared to talk about how you evaluate student progress.
- Emphasize continued learning: Discuss professional development activities you've undertaken.

Example question: "How do you incorporate technology into your teaching to enhance student learning?"

5. Retail and Customer Service

- Emphasize customer-focus: Provide examples of how you've gone above and beyond for customers.
- Showcase sales skills: Be prepared to discuss your sales achievements and techniques.
- Highlight conflict resolution: Discuss how you've handled difficult customer situations.
- Demonstrate adaptability: Retail environments can be fast-paced and changeable, so emphasize your flexibility.
- Discuss teamwork: Retail often involves working closely with others, so

highlight your collaborative skills.

Example question: "Tell me about a time when you turned a dissatisfied customer into a loyal one."

6. Marketing and Advertising

- Showcase creativity: Be prepared to discuss innovative campaigns you've worked on.
- Demonstrate data analysis skills: Discuss how you use data to inform marketing strategies.
- Highlight digital marketing knowledge: Be familiar with current digital marketing trends and tools.
- Emphasize brand awareness: Discuss how you've successfully built or maintained brand identity.
- Show results-orientation: Be prepared to discuss specific metrics and ROI from your campaigns.

Example question: "Describe a marketing campaign you led that didn't meet expectations. What did you learn, and how did you apply those lessons?"

7. Legal

- Demonstrate analytical thinking: Be prepared to discuss complex legal issues you've handled.
- Showcase research skills: Highlight your ability to conduct thorough legal research.
- Emphasize attention to detail: Discuss how you ensure accuracy in legal documents.

- Highlight ethical considerations: Be prepared to discuss how you handle ethical dilemmas.
- Show client management skills: Discuss how you communicate complex legal issues to clients.

Example question: "Describe a situation where you had to explain a complex legal concept to a non-legal audience. How did you approach this?"

8. Manufacturing and Engineering

- Demonstrate technical knowledge: Be prepared to discuss specific processes and technologies relevant to the role.
- Highlight problem-solving skills: Provide examples of how you've optimized processes or solved engineering challenges.
- Emphasize safety awareness: Discuss your commitment to workplace safety and any relevant certifications.
- Showcase project management: Highlight your experience managing complex projects or teams.
- Discuss continuous improvement: Emphasize your commitment to efficiency and quality improvement.

Example question: "Describe a time when you implemented a process improvement that significantly increased efficiency or reduced costs."

9. Non-Profit and Social Services

- Demonstrate passion for the cause: Show genuine interest in the organization's mission.
- Highlight resource management: Discuss how you've maximized limited

resources.
- Showcase fundraising skills: If relevant, discuss successful fundraising initiatives you've been involved in.
- Emphasize community engagement: Highlight your experience working with diverse communities.
- Discuss impact measurement: Be prepared to talk about how you measure and report on program outcomes.

Example question: "How do you balance the need to serve beneficiaries with the demands of funders and stakeholders?"

10. Government and Public Sector

- Demonstrate knowledge of public policy: Be familiar with relevant policies and regulations.
- Highlight public service motivation: Discuss your commitment to serving the public interest.
- Showcase stakeholder management: Discuss how you've worked with diverse stakeholders.
- Emphasize transparency and accountability: Highlight your commitment to ethical conduct in public service.
- Discuss efficiency in bureaucratic settings: Provide examples of how you've improved processes in complex organizations.

Example question: "Describe a situation where you had to balance public interest with budgetary constraints. How did you approach this challenge?"

Conclusion

Tailoring your interview approach to the specific industry not only demonstrates your knowledge and preparation but also shows your genuine interest in the sector. Remember to:

- Research industry-specific trends and challenges before the interview.
- Prepare examples and anecdotes that highlight your relevant skills and experiences.
- Be ready to discuss industry-specific terminologies and concepts.
- Show enthusiasm for the industry and stay updated on its latest developments.

By customizing your approach, you'll be better equipped to showcase how your unique skills and experiences make you the ideal candidate for the role, no matter what industry you're targeting. Remember, the key is to demonstrate not just your qualifications, but also your understanding of and passion for the specific sector you're entering.

Chapter 19: The Power of Mock Interviews: Practice Makes Perfect

Mock interviews are one of the most effective tools in your interview preparation arsenal. They provide a safe environment to practice your responses, refine your communication skills, and build confidence. This chapter will explore the benefits of mock interviews and provide strategies for making the most of this powerful preparation technique.

The Benefits of Mock Interviews

1. Reduce anxiety and build confidence
2. Identify areas for improvement
3. Practice articulating your experiences and skills
4. Receive constructive feedback
5. Familiarize yourself with common interview questions
6. Improve your body language and non-verbal communication
7. Enhance your ability to think on your feet

Setting Up Effective Mock Interviews

1. Choose the right partner

Select someone who can provide honest, constructive feedback. This could be:

- A trusted friend or family member
- A colleague or mentor
- A career coach or advisor
- A professional in your industry

2. Recreate the interview environment

- Dress as you would for the actual interview
- Choose a formal setting
- Use appropriate technology for video interview practice

3. Provide context
Give your mock interviewer information about:

- The job description
- The company
- Your resume and application materials

4. Set clear objectives
Decide what aspects of the interview you want to focus on, such as:

- Answering specific types of questions
- Improving your body language
- Practicing your personal pitch

5. Use realistic timing

Aim for a mock interview that's similar in length to what you expect in the real interview.

Conducting the Mock Interview

1. Stay in character

Treat the mock interview as if it were real. Avoid breaking character or asking for do-overs.

2. Use a variety of question types
Include:

- Common interview questions
- Behavioral questions
- Technical or skill-based questions
- Unexpected or challenging questions

3. Practice active listening

Pay attention to the questions and avoid rushing to answer.

4. Use the STAR method

For behavioral questions, practice using the Situation, Task, Action, Result framework.

5. Ask questions

At the end of the mock interview, practice asking thoughtful questions about the role and company.

Providing and Receiving Feedback

1. Immediate self-assessment

After the mock interview, take a few minutes to reflect on your performance. Consider:

- What went well?
- Where did you struggle?
- How did you feel during the interview?

2. Detailed feedback from your partner
Ask your mock interviewer to provide feedback on:

- Content of your answers
- Clarity and conciseness of responses
- Body language and non-verbal communication
- Overall impression

3. Specific areas for improvement
Identify concrete areas to work on, such as:

- Eliminating filler words (um, uh, like)
- Improving eye contact
- Providing more detailed examples
- Speaking more slowly or clearly

4. Positive reinforcement
Acknowledge what you did well to build confidence.

5. Review and reflect
If possible, record the mock interview for later review and self-reflection.

Types of Mock Interviews

1. General practice interviews
   Focus on common questions and overall interview skills.

2. Industry-specific interviews
   Tailor questions to your specific field or role.

3. Behavioral interviews
   Emphasize STAR method responses to past experiences.

4. Technical interviews
   Include problem-solving or skill demonstration components.

5. Stress interviews
   Practice handling unexpected or challenging questions.

6. Video interview practice
   Focus on technology use and on-camera presence.

Maximizing the Benefits of Mock Interviews

1. Start early
   Begin practicing well before your actual interview to allow time for improvement.

2. Practice regularly
   Aim for multiple mock interviews to track progress and build confidence.

3. Vary your partners
   Different interviewers can provide diverse perspectives and feedback.

4. Gradually increase difficulty
   Start with basic questions and progress to more challenging scenarios.

5. Focus on improvement, not perfection
Use each mock interview as a learning opportunity.

6. Practice follow-up
Include post-interview elements like thank-you notes in your mock interview process.

Advanced Mock Interview Techniques

1. Role reversal
Take turns being the interviewer to gain perspective on what employers are looking for.

2. Panel mock interviews
Practice with multiple interviewers to prepare for panel interview scenarios.

3. Progressive interviews
Conduct a series of mock interviews, each focusing on a different aspect of the interview process.

4. Industry expert interviews
If possible, practice with someone in your target industry for highly relevant feedback.

5. Recorded sessions
Use video recording to analyze your verbal and non-verbal communication in detail.

Overcoming Common Mock Interview Challenges

1. Feeling awkward or self-conscious
Remember that feeling uncomfortable is part of the process. It's better to

work through these feelings in a mock interview than in the real thing.

2. Lack of realism
Try to create as realistic an environment as possible, including dressing appropriately and using formal language.

3. Difficulty finding partners
Consider using online platforms that offer mock interview services or joining professional networking groups.

4. Receiving overly positive feedback
Encourage your mock interviewer to provide honest, constructive criticism. Emphasize that you're looking for areas of improvement.

5. Overpreparation leading to scripted responses
While preparation is key, also practice being flexible and authentic in your responses.

Conclusion

Mock interviews are a powerful tool in your interview preparation toolkit. They provide a safe space to practice, receive feedback, and refine your interview skills. By engaging in regular, focused mock interview sessions, you can significantly improve your performance and confidence for the real interview.

Remember, the goal of mock interviews is not to memorize perfect answers, but to become comfortable with the interview process, improve your ability to articulate your experiences and skills, and build confidence in your abilities. With consistent practice and thoughtful reflection, you'll be well-prepared to shine in your actual interview.

As you continue your interview preparation, use mock interviews as a cornerstone of your strategy. Combined with thorough research, a strong understanding of your own qualifications, and a positive attitude, mock interviews can give you the edge you need to land your dream job.

Chapter 20: Beyond the Job Offer: Evaluating Opportunities and Making Smart Decisions

Receiving a job offer is exciting, but it's crucial to approach this final stage of the job search process with careful consideration. This chapter will guide you through evaluating job opportunities holistically and making informed decisions that align with your career goals and personal values.

1. The Importance of Thoughtful Evaluation

While it's tempting to immediately accept an offer, especially after a long job search, taking the time to evaluate the opportunity thoroughly can lead to better long-term career satisfaction. Consider:

- Your career trajectory
- Personal and professional growth opportunities
- Work-life balance
- Company culture fit
- Long-term financial implications

2. Key Factors to Consider

CHAPTER 20: BEYOND THE JOB OFFER: EVALUATING OPPORTUNITIES...

a) Compensation Package

- Base salary
- Bonuses and profit-sharing
- Stock options or equity
- Retirement benefits
- Health insurance and other benefits

b) Growth Opportunities

- Career advancement potential
- Professional development programs
- Mentorship opportunities
- Exposure to new skills or technologies

c) Company Culture and Values

- Mission and vision alignment
- Work environment
- Diversity and inclusion initiatives
- Corporate social responsibility

d) Work-Life Balance

- Typical work hours
- Flexibility (remote work, flexible hours)
- Vacation and personal time off policies
- Parental leave policies

e) Job Responsibilities and Challenges

- Alignment with your skills and interests
- Level of autonomy and decision-making power
- Potential for impact within the organization

f) Company Stability and Future Prospects

- Financial health of the company
- Industry trends and market position
- Growth projections and strategic plans

g) Location and Commute

- Commute time and transportation options
- Cost of living in the area
- Relocation requirements, if applicable

h) Team Dynamics

- Relationship with potential manager
- Team size and structure
- Collaboration opportunities

3. Gathering Additional Information

If you need more details to make an informed decision:

CHAPTER 20: BEYOND THE JOB OFFER: EVALUATING OPPORTUNITIES...

- Request a follow-up conversation with the hiring manager
- Ask to speak with potential teammates
- Research the company thoroughly (financial reports, news articles, employee reviews)
- Utilize your professional network for insights

4. Evaluating Multiple Offers

When comparing multiple offers:

- Create a pros and cons list for each opportunity
- Assign weights to different factors based on their importance to you
- Consider both short-term benefits and long-term career impact
- Don't focus solely on salary; consider the total compensation package and growth potential

5. Negotiation Considerations

Remember that receiving an offer often opens the door for negotiation. Consider:

- Market value for the role and your experience level
- Your unique skills and what you bring to the table
- Non-salary elements that could be negotiated (e.g., flexible work arrangements, professional development budget)

6. Handling Counteroffers

If you receive a counteroffer from your current employer:

- Evaluate why you were looking for a new opportunity in the first place
- Consider whether the issues prompting your job search will be resolved
- Be cautious of potential changes in your relationship with your current employer

7. Making the Decision

When you're ready to make a decision:

- Trust your instincts, but back them up with logical analysis
- Consider seeking advice from mentors or trusted colleagues
- Ensure the decision aligns with your long-term career goals and personal values

8. Accepting or Declining an Offer

When accepting an offer:

- Express enthusiasm and gratitude
- Confirm key details in writing (start date, salary, job title)
- Clarify any final questions or concerns

When declining an offer:

- Be prompt and professional in your communication
- Express appreciation for the opportunity

- Provide a brief, positive reason for your decision
- Leave the door open for future opportunities if appropriate

9. Navigating the Transition

Once you've accepted an offer:

- Give appropriate notice to your current employer
- Maintain professionalism during your notice period
- Begin preparing for your new role (e.g., researching, skill-building)
- Plan your knowledge transfer and exit strategy from your current role

10. Learning from the Process

Regardless of the outcome, reflect on the job search and decision-making process:

- What did you learn about your priorities and values?
- How can you improve your job search strategy in the future?
- What skills or experiences would make you more competitive for future opportunities?

Case Study: Evaluating Competing Offers

Sarah, a marketing professional with 5 years of experience, receives two job offers:

Offer A:

- Larger, established company
- 15% higher salary than current role
- Traditional benefits package
- Limited remote work options
- Clear path for advancement

Offer B:

- Smaller, growing startup
- 10% higher salary than current role
- Equity options
- Fully remote position
- Opportunity to build and lead a team

Sarah's Evaluation Process:

1. She creates a weighted decision matrix, assigning importance to factors like growth potential, work-life balance, and compensation.
2. She has follow-up conversations with both companies to clarify details about culture and long-term prospects.
3. Sarah consults with a mentor about the pros and cons of each opportunity.
4. She reflects on her long-term career goals and personal values.

Sarah's Decision:

After careful consideration, Sarah chooses Offer B. While the immediate salary increase is smaller, she values the opportunity for significant growth, the ability to shape a developing team, and the flexibility of remote work. The equity options also offer potential for greater long-term financial benefit.

CHAPTER 20: BEYOND THE JOB OFFER: EVALUATING OPPORTUNITIES...

Conclusion

The job offer stage is not just the end of your job search; it's the beginning of a new chapter in your career. By thoroughly evaluating opportunities, considering multiple factors beyond just salary, and aligning your decision with your long-term goals and values, you set yourself up for greater career satisfaction and success.

Remember, there's rarely a perfect job that ticks every box. The goal is to find an opportunity that aligns best with your priorities and offers a platform for growth and fulfillment. By approaching this decision-making process thoughtfully and systematically, you increase your chances of making a choice that you'll be happy with in both the short and long term.

As you move forward in your career, continue to reassess your goals and values regularly. The skills you develop in evaluating this job offer will serve you well throughout your professional life, helping you make informed decisions at every career crossroads you encounter.

Conclusion

As we conclude this comprehensive guide on acing job interviews, it's important to reflect on the journey we've taken together and the wealth of knowledge and strategies we've explored. The interview process is a critical juncture in your career path, serving as both a challenge and an opportunity to showcase your unique value to potential employers.

Recap of Key Concepts

Throughout this book, we've covered a wide range of topics, each crucial to interview success:

1. The Psychology of Successful Interviews: We delved into the mindset needed to approach interviews with confidence and authenticity.

2. First Impressions: We explored the power of dress, body language, and etiquette in making a lasting positive impression.

3. Company Research: We emphasized the importance of becoming an "insider" before you walk into the interview room.

4. Personal Branding: We discussed strategies for crafting and communicating your unique professional story.

5. Common Interview Questions: We provided frameworks for answering

CONCLUSION

typical questions effectively.

6. The STAR Method: We explored this powerful technique for structuring compelling responses to behavioral questions.

7. Showcasing Achievements: We learned how to quantify success and present accomplishments impactfully.

8. Addressing Gaps and Transitions: We tackled strategies for explaining employment gaps and career changes positively.

9. Asking Questions: We highlighted the art of demonstrating curiosity and engagement through thoughtful inquiries.

10. Different Interview Formats: We prepared for various interview settings, from one-on-one to panel interviews.

11. Virtual Interviews: We adapted our skills to the digital interview landscape.

12. Behavioral Interviews: We honed our ability to provide concrete examples of past performance.

13. Technical Interviews: We strategized on demonstrating expertise in specialized fields.

14. Salary Negotiations: We learned to navigate compensation discussions with confidence.

15. Follow-Up Strategies: We crafted approaches to leaving a lasting impression post-interview.

16. Handling Rejection: We explored turning setbacks into opportunities

for growth and future success.

17. Preparation Checklists: We created comprehensive guides to ensure thorough interview readiness.

18. Industry-Specific Tips: We tailored our approach to various sectors and roles.

19. Mock Interviews: We emphasized the power of practice in perfecting our interview skills.

20. Evaluating Opportunities: We learned to make informed decisions when faced with job offers.

The Holistic Approach to Interview Success

As we've seen, acing a job interview is not about memorizing a set of responses or following a rigid script. It's about presenting the best version of yourself, aligning your unique skills and experiences with the needs of the employer, and demonstrating your potential for growth and contribution within the organization.

The key to interview success lies in a holistic approach that encompasses:

1. Thorough Preparation: Research, self-reflection, and practice are foundational to interview success.

2. Authentic Communication: Honesty and genuineness create a connection with interviewers and showcase your true potential.

3. Adaptability: The ability to navigate different interview formats and unexpected questions demonstrates your versatility.

CONCLUSION

4. Confidence: Belief in your abilities, backed by preparation, shines through in your responses and demeanor.

5. Curiosity: Showing genuine interest in the role and company sets you apart as an engaged and motivated candidate.

6. Professionalism: From your attire to your follow-up, maintaining a professional approach leaves a lasting positive impression.

7. Resilience: The capacity to learn from rejections and persevere in your job search is crucial for long-term career success.

Beyond the Interview: Career Development

While this book has focused on the interview process, the skills and strategies we've discussed have broader applications in your career development:

1. Self-Awareness: The reflection required for interview preparation enhances your understanding of your strengths, weaknesses, and career goals.

2. Communication Skills: The ability to articulate your thoughts clearly and persuasively is valuable in all professional contexts.

3. Research and Analysis: The habit of thoroughly researching companies and industries serves you well beyond the job search.

4. Networking: The connections you make during your job search can become valuable professional relationships throughout your career.

5. Continuous Learning: The process of preparing for interviews in various fields encourages ongoing skill development and industry awareness.

6. Decision-Making: The skills used in evaluating job offers apply to many important career decisions you'll face.

The Ever-Evolving Job Market

As we look to the future, it's important to recognize that the job market is continually evolving. Technological advancements, economic shifts, and changing social dynamics all impact how companies hire and what they look for in candidates. Stay adaptable and continue to refine your skills and knowledge to remain competitive.

Some trends to watch include:

1. Increased emphasis on soft skills and emotional intelligence
2. Growing importance of digital literacy across all sectors
3. Rise of remote and hybrid work models
4. Focus on diversity, equity, and inclusion in hiring practices
5. Emphasis on continuous learning and adaptability

Your Ongoing Journey

Remember, your career is a journey, not a destination. Each interview, whether it results in a job offer or not, is an opportunity for growth and learning. Approach each interaction with curiosity and openness, always seeking to understand more about yourself, the industry, and the professional world at large.

As you move forward in your career, continue to:

1. Reflect on your experiences and extract lessons from each interaction

CONCLUSION

2. Stay current with industry trends and developments
3. Cultivate a strong professional network
4. Seek out mentors and be willing to mentor others
5. Set both short-term and long-term career goals
6. Regularly reassess and adjust your career path as needed

Final Thoughts

Acing a job interview is a skill that can be learned, refined, and mastered. With the strategies and insights provided in this book, you are well-equipped to approach your next interview with confidence and competence. Remember that each interview is not just a test of your qualifications, but an opportunity to explore how you can contribute to an organization and grow professionally.

As you embark on or continue your career journey, carry with you the knowledge that you have the power to shape your professional future. Your unique combination of skills, experiences, and personality is valuable. The interview process is your chance to showcase that value and find opportunities that align with your goals and aspirations.

Approach each interview as a learning experience and a stepping stone towards your ideal career. With preparation, practice, and persistence, you can navigate the job market successfully and find roles that allow you to thrive and make meaningful contributions.

Thank you for joining me on this exploration of interview success strategies. I wish you the very best in your career endeavors. Remember, your next great opportunity could be just one interview away. Go forth with confidence, authenticity, and enthusiasm. Your future awaits!

www.ingramcontent.com/pod-product-compliance
Lightning Source LLC
Chambersburg PA
CBHW071923210526
45479CB00002B/532